A Pocket History of Irish Traditional Music

GEARÓID Ó hALLMHURÁIN

THE O'BRIEN PRESS
DUBLIN

THE IRISH AMERICAN BOOK COMPANY (IABC)
BOULDER, COLORADO

First published 1998 by The O'Brien Press Ltd.,
20 Victoria Road, Rathgar, Dublin 6, Ireland.
Tel. +353 1 4923333; Fax. +353 1 4922777;
e-mail: books@obrien.ie website: http://www.obrien.ie

Published in the USA by
The Irish American Book Company (IABC)
6309 Monarch Park Place, Suite 101,
Niwot, Colorado 80503
Office: Tel. 303-652-2685; Fax. 303-652-2689
Orders: Tel. 800-452-7115; Fax. 800-401-9705

ISBN: 0-86278-555-3

British Library Cataloguing-in-publication Data
A cataloguing reference for this title is
available from the British Library

The O'Brien Press receives
assistance from

The Arts Council
An Chomhairle Ealaíon

Front cover photo: Martin Hayes by Helen Bommarito,
courtesy of Amy Garvey.
Back cover credits: top left, street scene by Ronan Quinlan; top right
traditional musicians from Clare and east Galway in the late 1940s
(from left to right) Seán Reid, Jack Cooley, Patrick Devenney, Tony
McMahon and Joe Cooley (courtesy of Séamus Mac Mathúna,
Cultúrlann na hÉireann); author's photo by Christy McNamara
Typesetting, layout, editing, design: The O'Brien Press Ltd
Cover separations: Lithoset Ltd
Printing: Cox & Wyman Ltd

CONTENTS

Introduction

INTRODUCTION

SHIFTING FORUMS AND CHANGING DEFINITIONS

A century and a half ago, the music collector George Petrie wrote that 'the music of Ireland has hitherto been the exclusive property of the peasantry. The upper classes are a different race – a race who possess no national music; or, if any, one essentially different from that of Ireland. They are insensitive to its beauty, for it breathed not their feelings; and they resigned it to those from whom they took everything else. He who would add to the stock of Irish melody must seek it, not in the halls of the great, but in the cabins of the poor.' The Great Famine, which provided the context for Petrie's observation, had a devastating impact on the topography of Irish traditional music. In its wake, the diaspora carried Irish music and song well beyond the rural cabins where Petrie transcribed during the middle decades of the last century. Since then, it has put down roots in the towns and cities of Ireland, and in Irish communities in North America, Europe and Australia. Its intriguing dispersal from the kitchens and crossroads of the West of Ireland to the concert halls and recording studios of the New World has been propelled further by the revolution in mass media, popular culture and international travel. While his music may be retraced to an historical rural dialect, a travelling piper, or an old gramophone record, the Irish traditional musician today commands the avid attention of a vast transnational audience.

There is no iron-clad definition of Irish traditional music. It is best understood as a broad-based system which accommodates a complex process of musical convergence, coalescence and innovation over time. It involves different types of singing, dancing and instrumental music developed by Irish people at home and abroad over the course of several centuries. Irish traditional music is essentially oral in character, and is transmitted from one generation to the next through a process of performance. Experienced musicians are capable of memorising up to five hundred pieces of music, some of which they play regularly, while others may lie dormant for years. While traditional music has developed largely beyond the literate process, much of it has been written down. Some performers learn formally from written sources, as well as informally from experienced players. Others learn from radio, television and sound recordings. Although its repertoire may seem conservative in form, the oral base of Irish traditional music allows it to be more fluid than written music.

Although some musicians and singers are folk composers in their own right, not all new compositions are accepted as part of the living tradition. When they are, the original composer is often forgotten and the tune absorbs the influence of different dialects, instruments and musicians. Hence, the multiplicity of versions of well-known tunes and songs which is commonplace in Irish music. Within the bounds of the established tradition, experienced performers use improvisation in their interpretation of tunes, songs and dances. This involves ornamenting and varying the basic melodic structures in dance music, as well as in traditional songs. Most musicians refer to their music as 'traditional music' or 'Irish music'. The term 'folk music' is only used on occasion, while labels like Celtic Music, World Music and the recent misnomer Afro-Celtic Music are marketing terms, which hold little or no merit among traditional performers.

THREE INTERLOCKING TRADITIONS

In older rural communities in the West of Ireland, music usually followed the work cycle of the agricultural year. Festivities began with the Wrenboy celebrations on St

Stephen's Day (shortly after midwinter), continued through the matchmaking and weddings of Shrove (which often involved four or five house dances) and on into the sowing and harvest seasons, until the cycle began again. Traditional music today has moved beyond this older milieu and may be heard at social gatherings, pub sessions, dances, concerts and festivals in various urban settings.

Irish instrumental music is sometimes referred to in terms of regional styles. A fiddler may be described as having a Sligo, Clare or Donegal style. While these simple county divisions are valid to a degree, research among some older communities in the West of Ireland has revealed a more precise topography of musical dialects. Many of these are based on older *clachán*-type communities (rural clusters of extended kin and neighbours) which have remained intact since the post-famine era and are distinguished by specific dance rhythms, repertoires and other features.

The most common dance tunes in the Irish tradition are reels, jigs, hornpipes, polkas, slides, mazourkas and highlands. Slow airs (usually based on *sean nós* songs in Irish) are also played by many instrumentalists. These sound most authentic when played on uilleann pipes, fiddle, flute or tin whistle. Dance tunes usually consist of two eight-bar segments which older musicians refer to as 'the first part' and 'the turn'. Each part is played twice through and the sequence is repeated twice (or three times) before changing into a new tune.

Most dance tunes in the Irish tradition date from the eighteenth and nineteenth centuries. They are played on various wind, string and free-reed instruments, including flute, tin whistle, uilleann pipes, fiddle, concertina and accordion. With the exception of the goat skin *bodhrán* (a traditional drum played with a stick) and drums used in céilí bands, percussion instruments are of minor

7

importance. Some of the most important developments in Irish fiddle music during the twentieth century took place in the United States, motivated by Sligo fiddlers Michael Coleman, James Morrison and Paddy Killoran. In Ireland, fiddlers Tommy Potts, Johnny Doherty, Paddy Canny and Denis Murphy have been responsible for some unique regional and stylistic contributions to their genre. Contemporary piping has been shaped ostensibly by the playing of Séamus Ennis and Willie Clancy. Their styles are endemic today in the playing of Robbie Hannon, Mick O'Brien, Ronan Browne and Jimmy O'Brien-Moran. Flute and whistle playing have been influenced by the recordings of John McKenna, John Joe Gardiner and Tom McHale, who in turn have inspired master performers Josie McDermott, Paddy Carthy, Mary Bergin, Eddie Maloney, Paddy Mullins, Catherine McEvoy and Carmel Gunning.

Accordions and concertinas have been the most prominent melody instruments in Irish traditional music since the 1950s. Notables like Joe Burke, Mary McNamara, Tony McMahon, Noel Hill and Sonny Murray have drawn extensively from the repertoires of masters like Joe Cooley, Paddy O'Brien, Paddy Murphy and Chris Droney. The banjo (originally an African instrument, brought to America during the slave trade) has also made its presence felt in the Irish tradition, especially in the hands of Barney McKenna, Kieran Hanrahan, Mick O'Connor, John Carty and Cathal Hayden. Harpers Máire Ní Cathasaigh, Michael Rooney and Janet Harbison have spurred a renaissance in Irish harp music. Other instruments have also been brought into the Irish music fold, among them the piano, mouth organ and piano accordion. The notables in this domain include Felix Dolan, Geraldine Cotter, Karen Tweed, Eddie Clarke, the Murphy Family, Brendan Power and Jimmy Keane. Despite the obvious antiquity of the dance music, folk composers like Paddy Fahy and Junior Crehan continue to turn out new tunes. Similarly, compositions by Seán Ryan, Paddy O'Brien and Ed Reevy have gained respect within the tradition. Lilting (*portaireacht*) or mouth music has also regained its status in recent years. This was traditionally used for dancers in the absence of instruments at country house dances.

The song tradition in Ireland is determined largely by the two linguistic cultures on the island. The most archaic form is *sean nós* (old style) singing in the Irish language. Each regional dialect of Irish has it own unique *sean nós* style. A complex and magnificent art, *sean nós* is an unaccompanied form of singing which demands tremendous skill and artistic understanding. It derives in part from the bardic tradition of professional poetry which declined in the seventeenth century. There is no display of emotion or dramatics in *sean nós*. The singer is expected to vary each verse using improvisation, an implicit musical skill which requires subtle changes in rhythm, ornamentation and timbre. Among the most celebrated *sean nós* masters in recent times were Darach Ó Catháin, Seán 'ac Dhonncha and Seosamh Ó hÉanaí.

The transition from Irish to English language was marked by the growth of bilingual macaronic songs, many of which still survive. There are two categories of songs in English – English and Scottish songs; and Anglo-Irish songs. The first was introduced to Ireland by English and Scottish settlers in the seventeenth century, and by Irish migrant workers. This genre, which includes classic ballads like 'Lord Baker' and 'Barbara Allen', is still popular in Ulster and may be heard in the repertoires of Len Graham, Anne Brolly and Paddy Tunny, as well as in the recordings of Geordie Hanna, Joe Holmes and Eddie Butcher. Anglo-Irish songs were composed by Irish people whose mother-tongue was English. These songs address the themes of love, courtship, emigration, politics, elopements and other topics of human interest. The songs of Paddy Berry, Ann Mulqueen and Tom Lenihan fall into this category. Apart from these secular songs, a unique body of carols has survived in the village of Kilmore Quay, Co Wexford. It dates from the seventeenth century and derives from a corpus of songs published by Luke Wadding in Ghent in 1684, as well as a manuscript collection compiled by William Devereux in Wexford in 1734.

There are very few written accounts of dancing in Ireland before the eighteenth century. Foreign travellers have left vague references to the 'Irish Hey', as well as the 'sword dance', the 'round dance' and the 'long dance'. The English geographer Arthur Young left a perceptive account of the Irish dancing master in the late 1770s. Since then, Irish dancing has split into three distinct traditions, all of which derive from a common rural source. They comprise of set dancing, *céilí* dancing and step dancing, each of which has close cognates in North America. Michael Flatley's theatrical extravaganza *Lord of the Dance* derives much of its material from the formulaic step dancing initiated by Gaelic League revivalists in the late nineteenth century.

During the past decade, considerable media attention has been focused on Irish traditional music. Despite this exposure, however, its history is still obscured by deference, rhetoric and the conflicting currents of popular opinion. The purpose of this book is to shed further light on this immense reserve of Irish social history, to acknowledge the music makers who have sustained it, and to delight in their *draíocht* on the eve of a new millennium.

Gearóid Ó hAllmhuráin
San Francisco, 1998

MUSIC IN EARLY AND MEDIAEVAL IRELAND

Popular media today has become fascinated with what is vaguely termed 'Celtic Music'. This World Music genre has evolved in recent times from the traditional musics of Ireland, Scotland, Wales and Brittany. It has also been influenced by the traditional music of the Irish and Scottish diasporas throughout North America since the late 1700s. Modern Celtic music, however, has no historical basis whatever in the music of the ancient Celts.

MUSICIANS AND DANCERS IN CELTIC SOCIETY

The Celts arrived in Ireland from mainland Europe in the fifth century BC. Imposing their civilisation on their predecessors through warfare and conquest, these Iron Age warriors have left few traces of their own music, songs or dances. What little is known has been gleaned from the writings of Classical historians and from scattered artefacts on the European mainland. Excavations of Celtic sites in Hungary suggest that the lyre was popular among the earliest Halstatt Celts. Later, the Celts of Gaul played music on U-shaped lyres which were represented on Gaulish coins. Dancing may also have been common among the Celts. Three bronze figures found in Loiret and Saint-Laurent-des-Bois in France depict naked Celtic dancers from the Gallo-Roman period. Further evidence of music among the Celts is provided by Classical writers such as Diodorus Siculus and Polybius. Both reported that the Celts used music in battle, while Diodorus described in detail the sacred role of the druids and bards among the Celts of Gaul.

MUSICIANS IN EARLY IRISH SOCIETY

The settlement of several waves of Celtic invaders in insular Europe eventually spawned the Gaelic-speaking people of Ireland and Scotland. As the Roman Empire was giving way to barbarian invasions in the fourth and fifth centuries, these Gaels adopted Christianity and grafted it onto an archaic pagan world. With Christianity came Latin literacy and learning which was maintained by secular poets and monastic scribes. It is from these secular and monastic scholars that we get the first indirect accounts of musicians in Early and Mediaeval Ireland. These 'patriarchal' historians describe only the male performers of the period, although it is most likely that women performers were also popular in Early Ireland.

While their music was non-literate and therefore beyond the scope of the scribe, the earliest written references to musicians in the Old Irish sources occur in the Brehon Laws. One of the most informative of these tracts is *Crith Gabhlach,* which was written down towards the end of the eighth century. Focusing on social status, it refers explicitly to the legal standing of the *cruitire* or harper and places him above all other musicians in the social pyramid. Beneath him was a rabble of unfree musicians referred to as 'singers of *crónán',* jugglers, mummers and buffoons, who had no legal franchise beyond that of the patrons who kept them. Although he was considered inferior to the poet, the harper was considered a freeman and enjoyed the same rights as smiths, physicians and other skilled craftsmen. Higher up the social pyramid, the harp and *timpán* teacher (a stringed instrument sounded with a bow) enjoyed the same standing as the *bó-aire* or strong farmer. Both had a legal honour price of four cows. There is little doubt that the harper's superiority was guaranteed by his honoured role in the lord's retinue of brehons, poets and genealogists whose duty was to eulogise their benefactor and prolong his political clout. How else can we account for the laws referring to the *crann gleasa* or 'tuning key' of the harp, and the severe penalty prescribed for the culprit who borrowed it and failed to return it on time?

Musicians get further mention in the eleventh-century poem *'Aonach Carman'* contained in the *Book of Leinster*. The poem describes the fair of Carmen held near the Curragh, Co Kildare, once every three years on 1 August, to mark the Celtic festival of *Lughnasa*. The poem contains one of the earliest references to the pipes in Early Ireland. It distinguishes clearly between *píopaí* (pipes) and *cuisleannaigh* (pipe blowers), suggesting that different instruments and performers were involved. Various stringed and wind instruments are also mentioned, among them the *timpán*, a *fidil* (which should not be confused with the modern violin developed in Italy during the sixteenth century), a *buinne* (probably a horn-like trumpet), a *feadán* (whistle) and a *cuiseach,* which was possibly made of reeds and corn stalks.

HYPNOTIC MUSIC IN THE SAGAS

Musicians feature prominently in the early prose sagas, especially those which are contained in the four great collections or 'cycles' – the Mythological Cycle, the Ulster Cycle, the Fianna Cycle and the Kings Cycle. Transmitted orally for centuries before being written down, the sagas feature a full cast of kings, queens, champion fighters, druids, seers and musicians. They focus on the otherworldly powers of music which were divided into *geantraí,* the music of happiness; *goltraí,* the music of sadness; and *suantraí,* the music of sleep and meditation. Harp strings of brass, silver and iron produced each of these hypnotic states.

While the musician had an abundant repertoire of tunes to woo his admirers and satirise his enemies, instruments too could exact revenge on the command of their masters. In the story of the mythological 'Battle of Magh Tuireadh', which was fought between the Tuatha Dé Danann and the Fomorians, the Dagda (the principal deity of the Tuatha Dé Danann, who was renowned for his voracious appetite, generosity and music) set out to gain the release of his harper Uaithne, who had been captured by the Fomorians. Following the invaders to their camp, he spied the silenced harp hanging from a wall. He bade the harp come to him, which it did – killing no less than nine of the Fomorians on its way. The Dagda then played each of the three kinds of music for his unsuspecting audience, starting with *goltraí*, until all the women present wept bitterly, then *geantraí*, until the young people burst out laughing, and *suantraí* to plunge the whole assembly into sleep. He and his harper then escaped unharmed. Similar scenes of musical magic occur in other prose sagas. In the epic *Táin Bó Cúailnge* ('The Cattle Drive of Cúailnge'), where Cúchulainn and the men of Ulster clash with Queen Meadhbh of Connacht, and 'The Pursuit of Diarmuid and Gráinne', a tragic love story, a host of spell-binding bards and minstrels are all part of the action.

Music also had the power to defy death. In the mythological 'Battle of Almhaine', in which Ferghal Mac Maeldúin was defeated by the King of Leinster, the head of his minstrel Donn Bó continued to sing long after it was severed from his body. The saga recounts, early on, that Donn Bó's widowed mother was very proud of her son's good looks, music and cleverness. He was so popular that the Leath Chuinn army would not travel into battle without Donn Bó to entertain them. Mac Maeldúin appealed to the widow to let her son accompany his army. After several lengthy exchanges, she reluctantly conceded to let Donn Bó travel to Almhaine. Fortune however did not favour the brave in this instance. Both Ferghal and Donn Bó were killed in the battle that ensued.

That night, as the victorious men of Leinster were celebrating, their king, Murchadh Mac Briain, ordered one of them to go out and fetch him a head from among the slain. As the servant roamed the battlefield, he heard a voice proclaim: 'You have been commanded by the keening women to play music for your lords tonight.' After this eerie announcement, the unsuspecting warrior heard a harmony of beautiful instruments. The source of this magical music was Donn Bó's head which was fulfilling his promise to entertain his fallen king and compatriots. The head was then brought back to the Leinster camp, but refused to perform for its captors – unless it could face the wall, and avoid the embarrassment of facing its enemy. The sweetness of Donn Bó's *goltraí* overwhelmed the Leinstermen so much that they felt ashamed of their slaughter. They sent a warrior back to the battlefield to fetch the rest of Donn Bó's body. When he returned, the head was rejoined to the shoulders and Donn Bó, alive and well, made his way home to his mother.

MUSICIANS IN THE MONASTIC SOURCES

While the monasteries in Early Christian Ireland were primarily places of worship and scholarship, their keepers were hardly oblivious to music. Their high crosses and reliquaries, psalters and hagiographical manuscripts all recognise the musician. It is reasonable to assume that these communities sang psalms and other ecclesiastical offices. Even though no contemporary transcriptions survive, it has been suggested that the early Irish church had its own form of Latin chant which was possibly closer to the Coptic chant of Egypt than to Roman hymnology. In parts of the West of Ireland today, where *sean nós* singing still survives, it is believed that this unique form of modal singing in Irish was handed down from *amhránaíocht na manach sa tsean aimsir,* or from 'the chanting of the monks in olden times'.

The earliest iconographical representation of the triangular harp appears in the ninth-century *Psalter of Folchard.* This illustration, which shows the Ark of the Covenant and a crowned King David holding a triangular harp, was made for the Benedictine monastery of St

Gallen, Switzerland, founded by the Irish missionary St Gall in the early seventh century. Back in Ireland, both harps and lyres featured prominently on high crosses between the ninth and eleventh centuries. Containing scenes from the Old and New Testaments, these panels were used as teaching tools for the laity at a time when illuminated books were rare and literacy was confined to a minority of monastic scribes. In interpreting the Bible, it was natural that the masons would carve visual materials (including familiar musical instruments) that their audiences recognised. Hence, the prevalence of lyres, harps and pipes. The West Cross at Kells, Co Meath and the Cross of the Scriptures at Clonmacnoise, Co Offaly, both contain lyres, while the latter also includes a piper. Further south in Castledermot, Co Kildare, and Ullard, Co Kilkenny, harps adorn high crosses carved during the ninth century.

The stone mason who fashioned the Last Judgment scene on Muireadach's Cross at Monasterboice, Co Louth, also found a place for native musicians. This tenth-century depiction is located on the east face of the cross and is probably a portrayal of the music of the blessed and the damned – a common theme in mediaeval iconography. It has been suggested that the damned are represented by the musician playing the triple pipes which may have had evil connotations during the Early Christian period. The fate of the blessed is proclaimed by the lyre, on which a celestial bird is perched. The same heavenly bird motif is repeated on the plaque of St Mogue's shrine from the eleventh century. This ornate piece of metalwork from Drumlan, Co Cavan, shows a bearded figure playing an eight-string triangular harp with distinctly Irish features. On the top corner, a bird is perched in the same manner as its forerunners on the high crosses.

HARPERS IN THE PSEUDO-HISTORIES

By the time the Early Christian period was coming to an end in the eleventh century, Irish society was undergoing a series of political and cultural changes. By now, the patchwork of 150 small kingdoms which made up the political geography of Early Ireland had dissipated. In its place, a few powerful provincial kings were sparring for control over the whole island. The century and a half between the Battle of Clontarf in 1014 (where Brian Boru quelled the Danes and their Leinster allies) and the arrival of the Normans in 1169, saw an intensive artistic renaissance in Ireland. Much of this scholarship was propelled by the ambitions of the provincial kings. Their men of learning were compiling new pseudo-histories and endorsing rival claimants in the emerging feudal politics of the day.

One of the most dynamic pseudo-histories of the period was *Lebor Gabála Érenn,* 'The Book of the Taking of Ireland', which grafted the history of Early Ireland onto the story of Creation in the Old Testament. The book connected the people of Early Ireland to the descendants of Adam through Japheth, son of Noah, who in turn was related to the sons of Míl, the final wave of settlers to arrive in Ireland. The story claims that after travelling through Egypt, Crete and Sicily, the sons of Míl arrived in Spain where one of their kinsmen, Bregon, built a tower to survey the territory and the distant horizon. From the top of his tower, he saw Ireland and set off to investigate it. When he arrived, he aroused the suspicions of the Tuatha Dé Danann who killed him. His kinsmen, the eight sons of Míl, then invaded Ireland to avenge his death.

Musicians are also mentioned in this pseudo-historical fiction. In explaining the division of the country into two political camps (which reflected the twelfth-century rivalry between the Uí Neill in the north and the O'Briens in the south), *Lebor Gabála Érenn* accounts for the feud between Éremon, leader of the expedition from Spain, and his kinsman Éber. After arbitration was handed down to them by Amairgen, their poet and judge, Éber insisted on a division of the country between himself and his brother. Éremon then took the North and Éber the South. Before parting, the brothers drew lots for their artists – a poet and a harper. The poet, a 'learned man of mighty power', went north with Éremon, and the harper went south with Éber. Given the distinction between the poet and the harper in the law tracts, this schematic division of the country between the literate North and the musical South was a cunning assertion of artistic as well as political power.

GIRALDUS CAMBRENSIS AND THE NORMANS

By the late twelfth century, foreign powers were turning their attention towards Ireland. The first to set foot in the country were the Normans, who arrived in Wexford in 1169. Their arrival was preceded by the political misfortunes of Diarmaid MacMurchadha, King of Leinster, who sought the aid of the Welshman, Richard de Clare, in regaining his kingdom. This provincial scenario quickly led to a large-scale invasion of Ireland. After securing their positions along the east coast and midlands, the Normans went on to establish feudal government, expand town life, and fine-tune many of the changes which were already taking place in the native Irish church.

With the expansion of Norman government came an influx of new bureaucrats and historians. One of the most musically informed of these historians was the Welsh cleric Giraldus Cambrensis, whose family was involved in the conquest. Before coming to Ireland, Giraldus had studied law, philosophy and theology in Paris. As an educated cleric, he may have been familiar with Latin plainchant and polyphony as it was used in the liturgy, as well as the secular music of the feudal court. He first visited Ireland in 1183, and came back two years later as tutor to Prince John. In his *Topographica Hiberniae,* an account of his visit written in obscure Latin, Giraldus left a scathing description of the 'barbarians' he met in Ireland.

He rebuked them for their poor animal husbandry, their lack of industry and their disinterest in city life. Their love of liberty and leisure also incurred the wrath of his pen.

In the midst of his moral broadside, Giraldus left a wealth of information about native musicians. He admits that the quality of their playing was more agreeable than that which he heard in England: 'I find among these people commendable diligence only on musical instruments, on which they are incomparably more skilled than any other nation I have seen. Their style is quick and lively. It is remarkable that, with such rapid fingerwork, the musical rhythm is maintained and that, by unfailingly disciplined art, the integrity of the tune is fully preserved throughout the ornate rhythms and the profusely intricate polyphony.' This is the oldest surviving account of musical performance in mediaeval Ireland – a subject which native historians had ignored for nearly a millennium.

While the Normans did little to alter the role of the musician in early mediaeval Ireland, the longterm cultural changes which accompanied their conquest left an indelible imprint on Irish music. Within a generation of the first settlers, the Normans began to adopt Irish customs and eventually became 'more Irish than the Irish themselves'. They learnt the Irish language and Gaelicised their surnames. They intermarried with the natives and patronised their musicians. By the early fourteenth century, however, it became clear that the Norman conquest was destined to remain incomplete. The Bruce invasion from Scotland (1315-1318) wreaked havoc on the country from without, while racial assimilation between Norman and Gael was having its own withering impact from within. Eventually, the Crown took action in 1366 by passing the notorious Statutes of Kilkenny. Henceforth, Norman settlers were prohibited from using Irish laws, language and customs. There could be no alliance between Norman and Gael, either by marriage, fostering of children or concubinage. It also became an offence to entertain native bards, pipers and harpers 'since they spy out secrets'. The Gaelic Irish who were living in Norman communities were now required to speak English even among themselves, and the colonists were urged to take up archery as opposed to hurling and other Gaelic games. Despite their initial vigour, the statutes were a longterm failure and did little to curb the patronage of musicians by natives and foreigners alike throughout the following centuries.

One of the most significant musical consequences of the Norman conquest was the growth in popularity of *amour courtois* or courtly love songs. These new songs expressed profound human emotions and a love of nature. Borrowed from the troubadour poetry of France and Spain, they were assimilated into native Irish verse in the form of the *amhrán,* using stress metres as opposed to the more archaic syllabic verse of the court poets. The most celebrated of the Norman poets to write *amour courtois* lyrics was Gearóid MacGearailt, third Earl of Desmond (1335-1398). Remembered as 'Gerald the Rhymer', he was an active protagonist in the political affairs of both Ireland and France during the latter half of the fourteenth century. He also played a significant part in implementing the Statutes of Kilkenny. Ironically, after his death, the Geraldines, his extended Norman family, abandoned French in favour of Irish as a language of court.

COURT POETS, REACAIRES AND HARPERS

In the period 1200 to 1600, a vast web of bardic patronage extended throughout the Gaelic world, from Cape Clear off Co Cork in the south, to the Outer Hebrides off Scotland in the north. Within this cultural nexus, hundreds of noble families kept hereditary *filí* or bards who composed in a more modern literary language, called

Early Modern Irish. This was an intense period of poetic activity which was spearheaded by bardic schools maintained by families like the Ó Dálaighs, the Ó hUígíns and the Mac an Bhairds. In the absence of overall political unity, the professional bards were the cultural guardians and social interpreters of an expansive Gaelic order – eulogising the deeds of their patrons, recording their history, and voicing their political ambitions.

The fourteen-year formal education of the *file* or bard included rigorous studies in genealogy, law and history, as well as intensive training in the oral art of syllabic poetry. This rigid form was based on the number and arrangement of syllables in a line or stanza. When the qualified *file* was ready to begin his career at court, he either attached himself to one chieftain, or he moved freely among various patrons from whom he got hospitality, protection and a place of honour.

Harp music was a vital corollary to the delivery of verse at the Gaelic court. As with all official verse, the eulogies of the *file* were sung by a *reacaire* (reciter) who was accompanied by harp music performed by the court *cruitire* (harper). The *file* oversaw the performance from his place of honour at the lord's table. The *duanaires,* or family poem books, of the period have left no evidence as to the kind of music used by the *cruitire*. Music historian Breandán Breathnach has suggested that the chants may have had an ecclesiastical origin, given that the metres used by the *file* were derived originally from the Latin hymns of the early church.

DANCING IN EARLY AND MEDIAEVAL IRELAND

If Early Irish historians were selective in their accounts of music making, they regrettably chose to ignore dancing completely. History has left no account of dancing in pre-Norman Ireland. Given their love of poetry and music, fairs and festivals, it is most unlikely that the people of Early Ireland did not dance. To compound this issue further, there was no native Irish word for dancing. This is clear in the twelfth-century translation of the 'Passion of Saint John the Baptist' from Latin into Irish. In telling the story of Salome's dance before Herod, the Irish scribe had no native word to translate the Latin *saltavit,* 'she danced'. To solve his dilemma, he informed his readers that Salome excelled in *'fri lémenda ocus fri hopairecht',* 'feats of leaping and activity'. The two common words for dancing, *rince* and *damhsa* (derived from the English 'rink' and the French *danse*), were not used in Irish until the late sixteenth century.

It is noteworthy that the earliest reference to dancing in Ireland occurs in a song composed in the South of England in the fourteenth century. Although there is no evidence to associate the writer of the song with Ireland, he does invite his listeners to 'come ant daunce wyt me in Irlaunde'.

If English rhymers were inviting dancers to Ireland, their Norman counterparts in Ireland were helping to popularise dancing through the medium of French (and later English) carol dances. The mediaeval carol was a group dance or choral performed in a ring. The dance leader sang the verses and the group responded with the refrain. Carolling was a favourite past-time among all classes in the Norman towns during the thirteenth and fourteenth centuries. It is probable that the earliest Irish square and round dances derived directly from these Norman imports.

The earliest written evidence for dancing among the native Irish is found in a report of a visit made by the Mayor of Waterford to the home of the O'Driscolls in Baltimore, West Cork, on Christmas Eve, 1413. On that auspicious occasion, the Mayor, along with the O'Driscoll and his son, as well as the prior of the local friary, all 'took to the floor' to celebrate Christmas in style.

PROFILE: THE BRIAN BORU HARP

The oldest surviving Irish harp is housed today in Trinity College Dublin. Although it has been nicknamed 'the Brian Boru harp', possibly because of its antiquity, it actually dates from the fourteenth century – three centuries after Brian Boru's death. It is about seventy centimetres in height and was strung originally with thirty brass strings which gave it a range of four octaves. It was played with long fingernails in the old Irish style. Music historian and harper Joan Rimmer has suggested that this harp may have produced the kind of music that Giraldus Cambrensis heard when he came to Ireland in the twelfth century. Used as the model for the national emblem depicted on Irish coins and official government stationery, the Brian Boru harp is one of the few instruments which have survived intact from mediaeval times.

TUDOR AND STUART IRELAND

By the early 1500s, Ireland was cluttered with the remains of previously uncompleted conquests as the Anglo-Norman lordship was whittled down to the Pale (the twenty mile radius around Dublin), and Hiberno-Norman families like the Butlers, Burkes and Geraldines were assimilated into the Gaelic order. The revolt of Silken Thomas, son of the ninth Earl of Kildare, in 1534, provided Henry VIII of England with an opportunity to destroy Geraldine supremacy in Ireland, and extend his writ over the whole country. Fearing that Spain might use Ireland as a base to attack England, and driven by a desire to exploit the commercial potential of the island, the four Tudor sovereigns (Henry VIII, Edward VI, Mary and Elizabeth I) finally completed the conquest of Ireland which had begun four centuries previously.

In 1541, Henry VIII became the first English monarch to declare himself King of Ireland. His reign, which was marked by the Anglican Reformation and the feudal subjugation of Old English lords and native Irish chiefs, had a profound impact on the cultural and political life of the island. Henceforth, the Catholic faith, which was shared by Norman and Gael, was purged of its possessions, while the king's 'Irish enemies' and 'English rebels' were obliged to accept English customs, laws and language.

HENRY VIII'S PROHIBITION OF IRISH MUSIC

Native musicians and literati also fell foul of the king's writ. Early in his reign, Henry VIII realised that the musician wielded no small share of political power. Consequently, he decreed that music and poetry were to be ruthlessly attacked, and that harps and 'organs' were to be destroyed, as they were inciting the natives to revolt. Another statute in 1533 suppressed the activities of the rhymer, the *píobaire* (piper), the bard, and the *aois ealadhn* (the artistic class). It was believed that by singing praises to 'gentilmen of the English Pale', Irish musicians were allegedly spreading 'a talent of Irishe disposicion and conversation' among the English gentry.

Despite his misgivings about native artists, Henry VIII found room for Irish pipers in the Tudor military establishment. Pipers accompanied the Irish kernes (professional soldiers) who were employed by Henry VIII in his campaigns against the Scots and the French. Similarly, Irish pipers were present at the siege of Boulogne in 1544.

THE ELIZABETHAN CONQUEST

The Elizabethan conquest grew out of a conflict between two disparate civilisations – one, a centralised Renaissance state bent on colonial expansion; the other, a Gaelic world characterised by an oral culture and widespread political fragmentation. While Elizabethan adventurers were busy 'discovering' the New World and imposing order on its indigenous peoples, their cohorts in Dublin were busy imposing order on Ireland – an untamed territory, which lay beyond the perimeter of Renaissance Europe. In an effort to curb the cultural autonomy of the natives (as well as impose her own political order on the island), Elizabeth I passed a number of decrees aimed at curtailing the influence of poets and music makers. Reacting strongly to Irish intransigence towards the end of her reign, she decreed that bards and harpers were to be executed whenever found. Such callous legislation, however, only served to bolster the role of the musician as a custodian of native culture. It also reinforced the power of music to represent a distinct Irish identity in opposition to Elizabethan occupation of the island.

ELIZABETHAN LITERATI ON IRISH MUSIC

To fulfill her political and cultural ambitions, Elizabeth brought a new coterie of bureaucrats and administrators to Ireland, among them celebrated literati like Edmund Spenser, Fynes Moryson and William Camden. Pioneer antiquarians in their own right, they recorded their impressions of Irish culture and geography in works like Spenser's *A View of the Present State of Ireland*, Moryson's *Itinerary*, Derricke's *Image of Ireland*, and Camden's *Britannia Sive: Angliae, Scotiae, Hiberniae*. They also found time to comment on the role of music and dancing. Moryson, who was secretary to Lord Mountjoy in the early 1600s, left a colourful account of the native Irish dancing dangerously with 'naked swords' in front of the Lord Deputy.

Spenser's work, which appeared in 1596, contained similar insights, as did Derricke's travelogue which was published in 1581. One of Derricke's woodcuts shows the *reacaire* (reciter) and the harper performing at the court of a Gaelic lord. Another of his woodcuts depicts the Irish kerne being led into battle by a piper, a fact which was confirmed by the Lord Deputy himself in 1572. Writing from Dublin about the frequency of rebel attacks, he complained to Elizabeth I that Fiach Mac Aodha Ó Broin, Rúairí Óg Ó Mórdha and other rebels were being led by pipers in the daytime and torchbearers by night.

'THE LAMENT FOR O'DONNELL'

Despite the fears of the Lord Deputy, the Pale withstood the incursions of Ó Mórda and Ó Broin. By the end of Elizabeth's reign, she had extended her power throughout the whole island through confiscation and plantation. Elizabeth's iron reign saw the routing of two Desmond rebellions, in 1569 and 1579, which were supported by Spanish and Italian allies. In 1588, the ill-fated Spanish Armada met its doom off the Irish coast. Survivors were quickly dispensed with at the end of a hangman's rope, as local sheriffs scurried to fulfill the queen's orders.

Despite Elizabeth's growing success, Ulster still remained the last political thorn in her side. In the late 1590s, native leaders like Hugh O'Neill and Red Hugh O'Donnell presented a formidable military challenge to Sir Henry Bagenal and the Earl of Essex, who arrived in Ireland in 1599. Their final confrontation came at the Battle of Kinsale in 1601. Out-manoeuvred by Mountjoy's army, O'Neill and O'Donnell, along with their Spanish allies, were heavily defeated and all the gains of their Nine Years' War quickly came to naught. This crushing defeat of the Ulster chiefs is remembered in the celebrated Munster air '*Caoineadh Uí Dhomhnaill*', ('The Lament for O'Donnell').

The Battle of Kinsale marked a watershed in Irish musical and literary history. Within a century, eighty-five percent of the land of Ireland was transferred to new English colonists and the old Gaelic order, with its traditional system of artistic patronage, had vanished forever. In 1607 Rory O'Donnell, brother of Red Hugh, and ninety other Ulster chiefs hoisted their sails in Lough

Swilly, Co Donegal and sailed into voluntary exile on the European mainland. Their retinues included scores of native poets and harpers, many of whom contributed to the Counter Reformation in the university towns of Europe during the seventeenth century. With this exodus, Ireland's tangled destiny as England's first colony was finally sealed.

The Flight of the Earls deprived the remaining literati and music makers of patronage. Throughout the seventeenth century, the archaic triumvirate of *file, reacaire* and *cruitire* crumbled. As the hereditary *file* was superseded by more plebeian bards (who were often reviled as makers of *camdhuan,* or crooked verse), he became more itinerant, and the process of composition, recitation and accompaniment now became the preserve of the solo artist.

MUSIC OF THE NEW PLANTERS

The plantation of Ulster now began in earnest. The process, masterminded by Sir Arthur Chichester, saw thousands of natives driven off 500,000 acres of prime land in Tyrone, Derry, Antrim and Armagh. In the wake of the clearances, the province was planted by Lowland Scots, many of whom were Gaelic-speaking Presbyterians from Galloway and Argyle. Apart from placing a wedge between the Gaels of Highland Scotland and their cultural cohorts in Ireland, the plantation nurtured the seeds of sectarian bitterness between evicted natives and incoming settlers. Ironically, it also introduced new music-makers to northeast Ulster. Apart from their eventual predilection for the fife and drum, Ulster-Scots settlers brought jigs and weavers' ballads with them to Ireland. Ironically, many of their dance tunes were similar to those enjoyed by their dispossessed neighbours. Their espousal of English culture facilitated the dispersal of ballad sheets and chapbooks containing popular English and Scottish ballads.

'THE LAMENT FOR EOGHAN RUA Ó NEILL'

Just as traditional music reflected the Tudor conquest in the 1500s, so too did it mirror the turbulent politics and religious disaffection of the 1600s. The first popular revolt against the Stuart regime in Ireland took place in 1641. It was led by a rebel assembly known as the Confederation of Kilkenny. This comprised of Old English and native Irish Catholics who were united in common cause against the New English colonists, most of whom were Protestant.

One of the masterminds of the 1641 rebellion was Eoghan Rua Ó Neill (1582-1649), leader of the Ulster army. A member of the noble Ó Neill family of Tyrone, he spent his youth in the Netherlands and became a distinguished officer in the Spanish army. He returned to Ireland in 1642 and won a major victory over the English forces at Benburb in 1646. Three years afterwards, as Eoghan Rua prepared to cross swords with Cromwell's Roundheads, he fell ill at Cloughouter, Co Cavan, and died shortly afterwards. According to popular folklore, Eoghan Rua died from poison which was placed in his shoes by a woman before a banquet in Derry. After several bouts of dancing, the heat from his feet forced the poison into his bloodstream and he died several days afterwards. Eoghan Rua was immortalised by native poets and harpers, not least in the 'Lament for Eoghan Rua Ó Neill' composed by the blind harper Turlough O'Carolan.

Contemporary records dealing with the rebellion of 1641 refer to bagpipers in the service of the Confederate forces. The most prominent piping tune to survive from this era is *'Máirseáil Alasdruim'*, ('Alasdruim's March'). The piece was composed in memory of Alasdair Mac Colla, hero of the Wars of Montrose in Scotland, who was killed at the Battle of Cnoc na nDos, Co Cork, in November 1647. The march is a musical description of the battle rally, and the ensuing fight against the forces of Lord Inchiquin. It finishes with a series of laments for the slain Alasdruim.

'THE CURSE OF CROMWELL'

The rebellion of 1641 paved the way for the arrival of Oliver Cromwell in Ireland. Landing in Dublin at the head of a Puritan army in 1649, his nine-month mission was driven not only by conquest, but also by revenge. Intent on avenging the supposed massacre of Protestants by Catholic Confederates, Cromwell was determined to crush the royalist cause in Ireland, and exploit the island to reward his soldiers. His indiscriminate slaughter of the garrison and townspeople in Drogheda and, later on, in Wexford, has left an indelible imprint on Irish folk memory.

Cromwell's brutal resettlement transformed the land-owning aristocracy in Ireland. Above all, it removed the traditional distinctions between the native Irish and the Old English. The principal leaders of the rebellion forfeited all land and property rights to the Commonwealth, while another group had land reallocated to them in Clare and Connacht (hence, Cromwell's infamous rallying cry 'To Hell or to Connacht'). No natives were to be settled in western port towns, or within four miles of the sea. This was designed to separate them from incoming Protestant settlers and, at the same time, to deny them access to their Catholic allies on the European mainland. Catholic priests were outlawed. Those who remained active risked being hanged or transported to the West Indies, where thousands of Irishmen and women were sold into slavery and indentured service.

Musicians too filled the ranks of the unwanted masses exported to the West Indies by Cromwell's bureaucrats. On 15 January 1656, *The Minute Book of the Council of the Barbadoes* recorded that an Irish piper, Cornelius O'Brien, was to have 'one and twenty lashes on the bare back by the Common Hangman befor the Cage at ye Indian Town'. He was accused of inciting mutiny and disturbing the peace and was given one month to leave Barbados.

'SEÁN Ó DUIBHIR A' GHLEANNA'

Irish soldiers lucky enough to escape the curse of Cromwell opted for voluntary exile in Europe. Some, like John O'Dwyer of Aherlow, Co Tipperary, and his cousin, Colonel Edmund O'Dwyer, chose to fight for Spain in Flanders. Edmund, who commanded a brigade of five regiments against Cromwell, surrendered on terms at Cahir in March 1652 and was allowed to leave Ireland with 4,500 of his men. His cousin John was eulogised in the song *'Seán Ó Duibhir A' Ghleanna'* which is still popular in the *sean nós* repertoire.

> An sionnach rua ar a' gcarraig, Míle liú ag marcaigh,
> Is bean go dúch sa' mbealach, Ag áireamh a gé.
> Anois tá'n choill dá gearra, Triallfaimid thar cala,
> 'S a Sheáin Uí Dhuibhir a' Ghleanna, Chaill tú do chéim.

> *The red fox on the rock, A thousand shouts from the riders,*
> *And a woman on the roadside, sadly counting her geese.*
> *Now the wood is being cut down, We shall cross the seas,*
> *O Seán Ó Duibhir of the Glen, You have lost your lordship.*

MUSIC AND THE WILLIAMITE WARS

The accession of the Catholic King James II in 1685 did little to change the traumatic impact of Cromwell's confiscations in Ireland. James's pro-Catholic stance was most unpopular in England and Scotland. When William of Orange challenged him for the throne of England, Ireland (with the exception of the Ulster Scots) rose in favour of James and became embroiled in a bloody European war which was to have a profound impact on the political and cultural life of the island.

James arrived in Cork in March 1689 to the sound of bagpipers and dancing. The tunes 'The King Enjoys his Own Again' and 'Lillibulero' (despite its anti-Catholic sentiments) were reputedly popular among Jacobite pipers. The conflict began when James's army arrived in Ulster. After a fifteen-week siege, the walled city of Derry was relieved in late July when a relief ship broke through a Jacobite boom on the river Foyle.

In June 1690, William of Orange landed in Carrickfergus, Co Antrim, and immediately headed south. Both armies met at the river Boyne on 1 July 1690 (12 July in modern calendars). William's army of 36,000 men included Germans, Dutch, Danes and Huguenots as well as British troops, while James's mustering of 24,000 was made up of French and Irish troops. After a day of intense fighting, James fled the battlefield (which earned him the nickname *Séamus a' Chaca* – 'James the Shit' – in contemporary folklore) and William's force emerged victorious. The Williamite victory inspired a huge repertoire of Protestant marching tunes like 'The Boyne Water' which still enjoy currency in Ulster.

After the Boyne, James's generals withdrew to the Shannon, where Athlone and Limerick became their final strongholds. The Jacobite general Patrick Sarsfield held Limerick against a fierce onslaught. His daring attack on the Williamite siege train at Ballyneety near Dundrum, Co Tipperary, on 11 August 1690, was immortalised in the popular ballad 'Galloping Hogan' named after Sarsfield's scout Dónall Ó hÓgáin who defied the English convoy. William eventually returned to England, leaving the Dutch general Ginkel in charge of the army. The war dragged on into 1691 and Ginkel eventually crossed the Shannon at Athlone after a desperate struggle which is evoked in the piece 'The Bridge of Athlone'.

'AUGHRIM'S DREAD DISASTER'

The Battle of Aughrim which followed the fall of Athlone is one of the most immortalised military encounters in Irish traditional music. Remembered by poets and musicians as 'Aughrim's dread disaster', it prefaced the demise of Jacobite power in Ireland. All of the slaughter and desolation of Aughrim are captured in its battle lament *'Gol na mBan san Ár'*, ('The Crying of the Women in the Slaughter'). A piping piece, which survives on a late 1890s recording of the blind piper Mící Chúmba Ó Súilleabháin, it simulates the march into battle, the clash and fury of the fight and the crying of the women lamenting the slain in the wake of battle.

The second siege of Limerick was a last desperate act of the Jacobite army to halt Ginkel's offensive. After a month of resistance, Sarsfield decided to strike a bargain. Under the terms of the Treaty of Limerick, Sarsfield and 14,000 of his men were allowed to go to France. There they joined the services of Louis XIV and became known as the Wild Geese. Their departure from Limerick was lamented in the poignant elegy *'Marbhna Luimní'*, ('The Lament for Limerick'). Later on, their regimental valour on the battlefields of Europe was immortalised in songs like 'Clare's Dragoons', which extolled the bravery of Lord Clare's regiment at the Battle of Fontenoy in 1745.

While most Irish soldiers chose to follow Sarsfield into exile, others opted to continue the fight as outlaw *rapparees* (from the Irish *rápaire*, or half-pike, a common weapon of the period). One of the most legendary rapparees of the Williamite period was Éamonn Ryan from Knockmeoil Castle, Co Tipperary, who has been immortalised in the song *'Éamonn an Chnuic'*. An associate of Sarsfield's famous scout, Galloping Hogan, Ryan was of noble stock and was forced into outlawry as a result of a fracas with a tax collector. He and his men fought for the Jacobites in the war against William of Orange. A proclamation issued in 1702 offered a £200 reward for his capture. Tradition holds that he was slain by a friend who, despite his treachery, failed to collect the princely sum from the magistrates in Clonmel.

Ryan's love song *'Éamonn an Chnuic'* portrays him as

a Robin Hood figure charming his way into the home of his ladyfriend on a cold and wintry night.

'Cé h-é sin amuigh,
Go bhfuil faobhar ar a ghuth,
Ag réabhadh mo dhoruis dúnta?'

'Mise Éamonn a' Chnuic,
Tá báidhte fuar fliuch,
Ó shíor-shiúl sléibhte is gleannta.'

*'Who is that outside,
With passion in his voice,
Beating my bolted door?'*

*'I am Ned of the Hill,
Drenched, cold and wet,
After trekking through mountains and valleys.'*

FENIAN LAYS

Ballads based on the mythological exploits of Fionn Mac Cumhail were extremely popular in Tudor and Stuart Ireland. The stories were set down in poetic form and were sung at court assemblies and communal gatherings. These ballads or lays (*laoithe*) were based on the twelfth-century prose compilation *Agallamh na Seanórach,* 'The Old Men's Discourse', in which the pagan warrior Oisín came back from *Tír na nÓg,* or the Land of Youth, to accompany St Patrick on his mission around Ireland and tell him tales about the various places they visited.

The mythological hero of the lays, Fionn Mac Cumhail, was the leader of the Fianna Éireann (the soldiers of Ireland), an army maintained by the High King, Cormac Mac Airt. The exploits of Fionn and his men are recounted in the lays, which were usually sung in four-line verses. Their themes were full of magical encounters, exciting journeys to the Land of Youth, fierce battles with monsters, and mischievous elopements. Lays were sung by all classes in Gaelic society, from West Cork to the tip of Lewis on the Outer Hebrides. The last *sean nós* singers to sing Fenian lays in Ireland were recorded in the 1940s in Glencolmcille, Co Donegal. The tradition survived until recent years among the older Gaelic singers on the Outer Hebrides.

LAMENTS

Laments or *caoineadh* are probably the oldest form of song to have survived in Ireland. Among the more prominent religious laments are Marian songs, which recall the suffering of the Blessed Virgin. Referred to as *amhráin bheannaithe* (religious songs), they include 'Caoineadh na dTrí Muire', 'The Lament of the Three Marys', and 'Caoineadh na Maighdine', 'The Lament of the Virgin', the themes of which derive from mediaeval apocrypha. Music historian Hugh Shields has suggested that these *amhráin bheannaithe* may have been composed by Mendicant friars.

According to folklorist Breandán Ó Madagáin, four kinds of funeral and death laments survived past the seventeenth century. The first and most common type was the 'keen' performed by the *bean chaointe* or keening woman in the presence of a corpse. This type of keening was often a communal process and acted as a form of collective catharsis in dealing with the death of a loved one. The most celebrated of these is 'Caoineadh Airt Uí Laoghaire', 'The Lament for Art Ó Laoghaire', composed in 1773 and attributed to his poet wife Eibhlín Dubh Ní Chonaill. The second type was the *marbhna,* or bardic elegy, composed in syllabic metre by the *file* for his dead chieftain. The third category of death lament became popular after the decline of the bardic schools in the seventeenth century. This was a semi-learned *marbhna* composed in stress metre by poets like Aogán Ó Rathaille (1670-1728) and Dáibhí Ó Bruadair (1625-1698) who tried to prolong the traditions of the bardic poets. The fourth type was the death song, which still features in the *sean nós* repertoire. These recall tragedies and disasters, and are not sung as part of the funeral ritual. Antoine Ó Reachtabhra's *'Anach Cuain'*, which recalls a drowning tragedy in Galway in 1828, is one such lament.

LOVE SONGS

Love songs composed by anonymous poets dominated the folk *amhrán* from the late seventeenth century onwards. The vivid emotional language in these songs is particularly striking. The voice of the girl describing her unhappy love affair with Dónall Óg is a typical case in point:

> Tá mo chroíse chomh dubh le hairne,
> Nó le gual dubh a bheadh i gceárta,
> Nó le bonn bróige ar hallaí bána,
> Is tá lionn dubh mór os cionn mo gháire.

> *My heart is as black as a sloe,*
> *Or a black coal in the forge,*
> *Or the print of a shoe on white halls,*
> *And a black mood conceals my laughter.*

The intense voice of hopelessness and dismay in the final verse draws on a graphic reservoir of oral folk motifs:

> Do bhainis soir díom is do bhainis siar díom,
> Do bhainis romham is do bhainis im dhiaidh díom,
> Do bhainis gealach is do bhainis grian díom,
> 'S is ró-mhór m'eagla gur bhainis Dia díom.

> *You took east from me, and you took west from me,*
> *You took before and after from me,*
> *You took the moon and the sun from me,*
> *And my great fear is that you took God from me.*

CEARBHALL Ó DÁLAIGH

While many love poets passed quietly into oblivion, others left a colourful imprint on the folklore of the seventeenth century. One of the most celebrated of the romantic poets was the ubiquitous Cearbhall Ó Dálaigh from Pallis in north Wexford, who supposedly got the gift of poetry from the milk of a magical cow.

Bearing the name of the hereditary poets to the MacCarthy's of Cork, Ó Dálaigh's love affair with Eleanor Kavanagh of Clonmullen Castle, Co Carlow, was filled with cunning and intrigue. The story goes that she was promised in marriage to a wealthy suitor by her father, Sir Morgan Kavanagh. Cearbhall found out about the beautiful Eleanor and her impending marriage, and decided to pursue her. He got a job from a cobbler near Clonmullen, and when she sent for a shoemaker to make her wedding shoes, Cearbhall went along to measure her feet. According to one version of the folk tale, Cearbhall had a beauty spot on his chest. While he was taking her measurements, he allowed his shirt to fall open. She caught a glimpse of his beauty spot and immediately fell in love with him. Despite their romance, her father would not hear of his daughter marrying a poet. On the night of the betrothal party, Cearbhall arrived at the castle disguised as a beggarman. He managed to gain entry and entertained the assembly with tricks. When he was asked to play a tune on the harp, he played a magical *suantraige* (sleep music) and put the whole assembly to sleep. He then persuaded Eleanor to elope with him. Both escaped undetected from Clonmullen castle, but not before Ó Dálaigh had turned his horse's shoes backwards, to avoid being tracked by the angry father. The sixteenth-century air *'Éibhlín, A Rún'*, which an unknown poet addressed to his true love, has been incorporated into the saga of Eleanor and Cearbhall. The song suited the circumstances and mystique of the elopement and is still popular today.

DANCING IN IRELAND: 1500-1700

There are numerous accounts of dancing in sixteenth-century Ireland, especially in English sources. Reference is made to the 'Hay', the 'Fading' and the 'Trenchmore' as popular dance forms, although no details of how they were danced are given. The 'Hay', which was probably of French extraction, is generally associated with the term 'Trotting the Hay' and may have been the forerunner of the 'Irish Trot' which was popular in London theatre in the 1720s.

The first visual representation of dancing in Ireland is to be found on an engraved bone plate bearing the arms of the Fitzgeralds of Desmond. It has been dated to the first quarter of the seventeenth century. It shows five men dressed in short jackets and brogues doing some kind of group dance. The jig is first mentioned in 1674 in a moral controversy involving two clerics. The Archbishop of Dublin, Dr Talbot, was at loggerheads with Friar Peter Walsh, who was having a good time singing and dancing 'giggs and countrey dances' at the Harp and Crown in Dublin. Apparently, the good doctor was finding it difficult to reconcile Walsh's vows of poverty with his nocturnal antics in the local pub.

The English travellers Richard Head and Thomas Dinley also provide some interesting insights on dancing. Both attest to its popularity among the poorer classes in rural Ireland. Head, writing in 1670, pointed out that 'their Sunday is the most leisure day they have, in which they use all manner of sport; in every field a fiddle and the lasses footing it till they are all of a foam'. In 1681, Thomas Dinley reported that 'they are at this day much addicted (on holidayes, after the bagpipe, Irish Harpe, or Jews Harpe) to dance after their countrey fashions (that is) the long dance one after another of all conditions, master, mrs, servants.'

PROFILE: TURLOUGH O'CAROLAN (1670-1738)

Regarded as the most famous of the Irish harpers, Turlough O'Carolan was born in Nobber, Co Meath, in 1670. When he was a child, his father migrated to Connacht in search of cheaper land, and found work with the St Georges in Co Leitrim and the MacDermott Roes in Alderford, Co Roscommon, which was then an Irish-speaking district. Mrs MacDermott took young

Turlough under her protection and provided for his education. When he was blinded by smallpox, she made provision for him to learn the harp. Equipped with a horse and guide, he began his career as an itinerant harper at the age of twenty-one. For the next forty-five years, he travelled extensively, particularly in Connacht, and was patronised by Gaelic, Anglo-Norman and Ascendancy families.

At the age of fifty, O'Carolan married Mary Maguire and began farming in Mosshill, Co Leitrim. After his wife's death in 1733 he took to the road again, although her passing left him severely depressed. His lament for her is one his best-known poems. Unable to overcome his grief, he sought consolation in drink. His doctors warned him to stop, or accept the consequences. He followed their advice for six weeks but eventually broke down in a grocer's shop in Boyle, where he asked the shop boy for 'the smell of a glass'. In 1738, he fell ill and died at the home of his first patrons, the MacDermott Roes in Alderford (now Ballyfarnon). Tradition holds that he died holding a tumbler of whiskey in his hand but had no strength left to drink it. It was a pity, he said, 'that two such friends should part, at least without kissing'.

O'Carolan lived at a time when Irish society was experiencing major political and religious upheaval. The old Gaelic system of artistic patronage was on its last legs, while the forced conversion to Protestantism of Penal Ireland was gathering pace throughout most of the country. Astutely aware of his working environment, O'Carolan tailored his craft to suit the taste and status of his audience. His music contains an eclectic mix of Irish and non-Irish tunes, composed in a variety of dialects, from baroque to vernacular dance music. A collection of his work was published during his own lifetime. Like many of his predecessors, he eulogised the two great loves of his life, women and whiskey, in tunes like 'Bridget Cruise' and the celebrated 'Receipt for Drinking'.

Much of his baroque work was inspired by Italian composers like Corelli and Geminiani and dedicated to younger members of the Dillon family of Lough Glynn and the Burkes of Glinsk, both Norman families with 'modern' aspirations. His planxties (from *plearácha,* or praise pieces) for the MacDermott Roes and the O'Connors of Connacht evoke an older world of the bard and the *duanaire.*

JACOBITES, DANCING MASTERS AND THE PENAL ERA

The success of the Williamite cause in Ireland left ninety percent of the land in Protestant hands. The Irish parliament, by now entirely Protestant, set about buttressing the control of the Ascendancy in all walks of life. Protestant nonconformists and Catholics were forced to pay tithes to the established church, and a strident series of anti-Catholic penal measures were placed on the statute books. While laws penalising religious minorities had been common throughout Europe since the Reformation, Ireland's penal laws were unusual in that they were directed against the majority of the population.

Under the new penal code, Catholics were excluded from parliament, the army, the legal profession and government services, nor could they teach or maintain schools. It was deemed illegal to carry arms, to own a horse worth more than five pounds or to send children to the Continent to be educated. Catholics were not allowed to buy land, and leases were restricted to thirty-one years. Inheritance now became a complex issue. The eldest son was allowed to inherit the whole estate if he became Protestant. Otherwise, the holding would be divided among all the male heirs.

The musician, poet and singer found much to reflect upon during this perplexed era. In 1697, the Irish parliament passed an act banishing Catholic bishops as well as monastic and regular clergy. Later on, provision was made to register parish priests, on condition that they took an oath of allegiance and worked within the bounds of the law. Under such bleak circumstances, Mass-going became a precarious practice. The *sean nós* airs *'An Raibh tú ag an gCarraig?',* ('Were You at the Rock?'), and *'Caoineadh an tSagairt',* ('The Priest's Lament'), mirror the dangers of the period. The former appears to evoke the perils of attending open-air services at a Mass rock, while the latter recalls the anguish of an itinerant priest ministering to a rural congregation against a backdrop of religious intolerance and uncertainty.

'PILL, PILL, A RÚIN Ó'

Unable to bear the illegal burdens of a clandestine lifestyle, some priests converted to the established church during the penal era. The lament for the Donegal priest Fr Dominick O'Donnell, said to have been composed by his mother when he became a Protestant clergyman in 1739, is one of the best-known songs to have survived from the penal period.

> Crádh ort, a Dhoiminic Uí Dhomhnaill,
> Nach mairg ariamh a chonaic thú:
> Bhí tú 'do shagart Dia Domhnaigh,
> 'S ar maidin Dia Luain 'do mhinistir.
>
> *Woe to you, Dominick O'Donnell,*
> *Alas for anyone who ever saw you,*
> *On Sunday, you were a priest,*
> *And on Monday morning, a minister.*

HARP MUSIC IN THE BIG HOUSES

The century of peace that followed the Williamite wars saw most of the population living in abject poverty. The only exception was northeast Ulster, where the linen industry thrived under the direction of Huguenot refugees who had been banished from Catholic France. During this time, the last remnants of the bardic order survived as itinerant harpers whose main patrons were new Ascendancy landlords and a scattering of old Gaelic families who managed to retain their former holdings. By now, the music of some harpers had acquired the features of English and continental composers. Others retained an archaic style of Irish harping, playing with long crooked fingernails on wire-strung instruments. Although harper composers like Turlough O'Carolan were treated well in the Ascendancy homes of their patrons, their itinerant lifestyle was harsh and demanding. Travelling on horseback or on foot through all kinds of weather, they relied almost entirely on the generosity of their patrons, whose growing numbers of large houses dotted the countryside in the 1700s. Many harpers were blind and depended on a guide to lead them from place to place. Others were considered illiterate and marginal in a cultural milieu which was now dominated by the pompous pretensions of musical literacy, and the growing presence of the piano-forte, invented in Italy in 1709, in the parlours of their patrons.

When it became clear that the oral art of the harper was facing extinction, several attempts were made to preserve it. In 1730 the first 'Contention of the Bards' was held in Bruree, Co Limerick. Fifty years later, James Duggan, a rich Irishman living in Denmark, sponsored a number of harp festivals in Granard, Co Longford. As well as providing support for the harpers, these festivals created some public awareness for their plight and helped stimulate appreciation for their art. Another decade was to pass before the music of the harper found a literate collector. By this time however, it had lost its connection with the archaic world of Gaelic Ireland.

AISLING SONGS

While harpers struggled on the periphery of Ascendancy culture, dovetailing their work with the latest trends in classical music from Europe, other musicians were busy adding to an existing store of music and song. By the 1720s the Gaelic poets had come to accept their reduced status as clerics, farmers, pedlars and hedge schoolmasters. Although in Munster some poets continued to hold 'Courts of Poetry', their compositions were now more community oriented, and dealt with a range of the religious, legal and economic issues affecting life in the Irish countryside. In many cases, their poetry functioned as an implicit form of political journalism.

One of the last poets to receive patronage for his work was Sliabh Luachra poet Aogán Ó Rathaille (1670-1728). Patronised by the MacCarthys of west Munster, he was the leading proponent of the *aisling* vision poem in which the poet meets a beautiful woman *(a spéirbhean)* who claims that the native Irish will eventually triumph over their enemies. Although it was a literary and not a folk creation, the *aisling* became a popular form of song throughout the eighteenth century. One of the most celebrated *aislings* of the period is *'Úr Chill an Chreagáin'* composed by the south Ulster poet Art Mac Cumhaigh (1715-1774), a younger contemporary of Ó Rathaille.

A fhialfhir charthanaigh, ná caithear tusa i ndealramh bróin,
Ach éirigh 'do sheasamh agus aistrigh liom siar sa ród,
Go tír dheas na meala nach bhfuair Gallaibh ann cead réim
go fóill,
Mar bhfaighir aoibhneas ar hallaíbh do do mhealladh le
siansa ceoil.

Good generous sir, don't let yourself be thrown into sad
depression,
But stand up and come west along the road with me,

To that sweet land of honey where the English have
taken no possessions,
Where we can take pleasure in halls enticed by music.

While the love-sick poet is invited to enter a dreamland
between his own impoverished reality and the spirit world
of the *spéirbhean*, this *aisling* clearly refers to the political
injustice of the *Gallaibh* (the English, or foreigners, who
are also referred to as *clann Bhullaí* or Williamites by
aisling poets). These vision poems were set to airs which
were already well-known, and became immediately
accessible to the whole community. Another literary and
musical device which paralleled the emergence of the
aisling was the designation of allegorical names like
Caitlín Ní hUallachín, An tSeanbhean Bhocht and *Cáit Ní
Dhuibhir* to Ireland.

MUSIC OF THE JACOBITES

The Jacobite insurrections in Scotland in 1715 and 1745
attracted considerable attention in Ireland and their cause
was openly espoused by musicians and singers. Jacobite
poets like Seán Clárach Mac Domhnaill, Piaras Mac
Gearailt, Seán Ó Tuama, and Aogán Ó Rathaille were
resolute in their belief that the Stuarts would return to
restore the old Gaelic aristocracy and unchain Catholicism
from the burdens of the Penal Laws. (Naturally, their own
material circumstances would improve in this utopian
dream.) Songs like *'Mo Ghile Mear', 'A Chuisle na hEigse',
'Eirigh Suas'* and *'Rosc Catha na Mumhan'* are very clear
in their invocation of the Stuart cause. So too are piping
airs like *'Loch na gCaor'* which recalls the defeat at the
hands of Cumberland's redcoats at Culloden Moor on 16
April 1746. As Gaelic civilisation was being purged from
the Highlands, the Young Pretender was immortalised in
Ireland by poetic code names like *An Seabhac Siubhal,*
(the Roving Falcon), *An Buachall Bán,* ('The Fair Lad')
and 'The Blackbird'; the latter still survives as a set dance
title two centuries after Culloden. Likewise, Charlie's

exploits are enshrined in tunes like 'Jenny's Welcome to Charlie' and 'Bold Johnny Cope'.

EOGHAN RUA Ó SÚILLEABHÁIN

While many of the Jacobite poets contributed to the vernacular song tradition of the eighteenth century, few if any had a direct impact on the dance music of the period. The most prominent exception was the Kerry poet Eoghan Rua Ó Súilleabháin (1748-1784). Born outside Killarney, Ó Súilleabháin was educated at a local hedge school where he learnt Greek, Latin, Hebrew and English. He was also well-versed in Irish literature. He spent much of his life as a teacher and *spailpín* (migrant labourer) in various parts of Munster. His poetry, although conventional in thematic content, was extremely rich in its use of language and metre.

According to popular folklore, the rakish Eoghan was quite a womaniser, and he earned himself the eloquent nickname *Eoghan a' Bhéil Bhinn* (Eoghan of the Sweet Mouth). In 1776, he was press-ganged and forced to join the British army. Serving under Admiral Rodney in 1782, he took part in a naval battle between the British and the French fleets in the Caribbean. After the battle, he composed a poem in English praising Rodney's victory, expecting to gain his freedom from the navy in return. Rodney refused, but Eoghan, after a series of crafty schemes, eventually secured his release and found his way back to Kerry. His poem 'Rodney's Glory' went on to inspire the well-known set dance which continues to enjoy popularity among *sean nós* step dancers today. Similarly, his poem *'An Spealadóir'* is still sung to the air of 'The Cuckoo's Nest' hornpipe.

IRISH MUSIC IN ENGLISH COLLECTIONS

Although Irish traditional music was essentially an oral art, some of it found its way into English collections as early as the seventeenth century. The first Irish tune to appear in print was *'Cailín ó chois tSiúre mé',* ('I am a Girl from the

Banks of the Suir'), which bore the spurious Anglicised title 'Callino Casturame'. The tune, which was played to the same air as the later rebel ballad 'The Croppy Boy', appears in *William Ballet's Lute Book* as well as in the *Fitzwilliam Virginal Book*. Other Irish tunes appeared in Playford's *The Dancing Master* and Durfey's *Pills to Purge Melancholy*, both of which were published in London in the second half of the seventeenth century.

The first exclusive collection of Irish music was Neale's *A Collection of the Most Celebrated Irish Tunes*, published in Dublin in 1726. This included some tunes by Turlough O'Carolan, who was still alive at the time, as well as popular airs like *'Marbhna Luimní'*, 'The Lament for Patrick Sarsfield' and *'Táimse 'm Choladh'*, ('I am Asleep'), the latter of which was used in the ballad operas of the period. Two other collections appeared before mid-century – Wright's *'Aria di Camera'* in 1730 and the two-volume *Burke Thumoth Collection*, published in 1750. John Lee's two collections of music were published in 1774 and 1780. The second is of particular interest to traditional musicians because it contains tunes attributed to the Limerick piper Walker Jackson which are still played today. *Historical Memoirs of the Irish Bards* was published by Jackson in 1786. This contains an interesting appendix of dirges, among them the 'Lament for the Battle of Aughrim' and *'Gol na mBan san Ár'*. While the 1790s opened with the publication in Edinburgh of Brysson's *A Curious Selection of Favourite Tunes with Variations*, which included fifty Irish airs, the collection of the decade was to be Edward Bunting's *Ancient Irish Music*. Published in 1796, this seminal work was to set the tone for Irish collectors throughout the nineteenth century.

DANCING IN EIGHTEENTH-CENTURY IRELAND

Throughout the time of the Penal Laws, traffic between Ireland and the European mainland continued largely unabated. Many of the minor Catholic gentry sent their sons to the Continent to be educated, while smuggling helped to sustain trade channels between some Gaelic families and their commercial cohorts in France and Spain. This traffic also influenced musicians and dancers in rural Ireland. The modern violin, which traditional musicians renamed the fiddle, was introduced and with it a bevy of travelling dancing masters, who sold their steps to all classes of society.

The *rince fada* had been a popular group dance in Ireland since the mid-seventeenth century. A combination of dancing and marching, it was usually danced when the bonfires were lit on May Eve. It was danced in jig time and had no set music. The group could choose to pick a king and queen, generally the two best dancers, who were charged with carrying the May Eve garland and hailing the return of summer with the song *'Thugamar féin an Sambradh Linn'*, ('We brought the Summer with Us'). Until the end of the eighteenth century, when it was ousted by the new French dances imported by the dancing masters, it was customary to dance the *rince fada* at the close of private and public balls.

Another form of group dance in the eighteenth century was the cake dance. This was not a particular dance but a *báire* or session of dancing at which a cake was offered to the best couple. Pantomimic or action dances were also popular. In Connacht, *'Maide na bPlandaí'* ('The Planting Stick'), was a solo dance which mimicked the tilling, sowing and digging of the potatoes. The *'Gabhairín Buí'*, which imitated the 'Sword Dance' using a sweeping brush, was popular in Clare, while in Connemara, *'Damhsa na gCoinín'* ('The Rabbit Dance'), resembled the 'Cobbler's Dance', an acrobatic stunt performed by the dancer throwing his feet forward from a squatting position.

In 1780, the English geographer Arthur Young noted that 'dancing is very general among the poor people, almost universal in every cabin. Dancing masters of their own rank travel through the country from cabin to cabin, with a piper or blind fiddler; and the pay is sixpence a quarter. It is an absolute system of education. Weddings are always celebrated with much dancing.' Young, who travelled in Ireland from 1776-79, also noted the dances that were popular at the time. He says that 'besides the Irish jig, which they dance with a most *luxuriant* expression, minuets and country dances are taught, and I even hear some talk of cotillions coming in'.

While Young mentions jigs, minuets, country dances and cotillions, he makes no mention of reels and hornpipes. It would appear that these dances did not arrive in Ireland until the end of the eighteenth century. Although O'Carolan composed some early reels, it is likely that the reel in its present form was imported from Scotland. Sheet music, which appeared in Dublin in the 1790s, contained well-known Scottish reels like 'Miss McLeod', 'Lord McDonald', 'Miss Johnson' and 'Rakish Paddy'. Similarly, the modern hornpipe was probably imported from England around the same period. It was popular as a stage act in the English theatre and was usually performed in between acts and at the close of plays.

PROFILE: THE DANCING MASTER

Arthur Young was the first observer in eighteenth-century Ireland to mention the travelling dancing masters. It is likely that they emerged on the Irish scene shortly before Young arrived. They appear to have originated in Munster and were extremely popular in Kerry, where they worked in tandem with hedge schoolmasters.

Although flamboyant and pretentious at times, the dancing master considered himself to be a 'gentleman' and sought to instil this grandiose spirit in his pupils. Besides teaching dancing to all social classes, he also

47

taught fencing and deportment to the children of the gentry. His arrival in a village or rural *clachán* was usually met with great delight. He stayed in a community for a six week 'quarter'. Generally, he would lodge in a farmer's house and have the use of a barn or kitchen to teach his steps. In return for the use of the facilities, he would not charge the children of the host farmer. Alternatively, pupils brought the dancing master home with them for the night, and vied with each other for the honour. At the end of the eighteenth century, the fee for a quarter was sixpence. A half century later, the fee had risen to ten shillings a quarter in Kerry – five shillings for the dancing master and five shillings for the musician who travelled with him.

The rising step of the jig and the side step of the reel were the first two basic steps taught by the dancing master. If his pupils were slow learners, he tied *súgán* and *gad* (straw rope and withe) to their feet, so that they could distinguish the left from the right foot. Various jingles were used to teach the rhythm of the steps. Common tunes like 'Miss McLeod's Reel' and its jig cognate 'The Campbells are Coming' were used to accompany verses like:

> *Sín amach cos an ghaid agus crap cos an tsúgáin,*
> *Bain cnag as t'altaibh agus searradh as do ghlúnaibh;*
> *Síos go dtí an dorus agus suas go dtí an cúinne*
> *Is go mbris' an riabhach do chosa mara deacair tú do*
> *mhúineadh.*

> Stretch out the withe foot and withdraw the strawrope
> foot,
> Take a crack out of your joints and stretch out your
> knees;
> Down to the door and up to the corner
> And may the devil break your feet if you're not hard to
> teach.

The reputation of the dancing master rested not only on his ability to teach but also on his talent for inventing new steps. Solo dances based on reel, jig and hornpipe steps, as well as set or figure dances like 'St Patrick's Day', 'The Blackbird' and 'Madame Bonaparte' were all created by dancing masters from the end of the eighteenth century. Because of the skill required to dance them, solo dances were considered the *crème de la crème* of the dancing master's repertoire. They were reserved for his best pupils who would perform them on a platform made of a half door taken off its hinges. Group dances like the quadrille sets, which became popular after the Napoleonic wars, were taught to all pupils. They required less disciplined footwork than solo dances. Teaching them to large numbers of pupils of all abilities helped to sustain stable classes, as well as satisfy the communal desire for conviviality and courting.

Rivalry between dancing masters was common in rural Ireland. Although an itinerant, each master 'owned' a certain territory or circuit. When a rival from outside the circuit encroached on a resident's plot, he was expected to challenge him to a 'dance off'. This involved the two masters competing against each other, often on an upturned barrel in the village square. The victor was given free rein to teach in the district, while the loser was 'banished' to another territory.

MUSIC OF THE EXILES: 1700-1830

After a millennium of relative autonomy, the conquests of the Tudors and Stuarts spurred a series of forced migrations from Ireland. When the Elizabethans deprived the Gaelic aristocracy of their former status in the early seventeenth century, they fled to the Catholic monarchies of Europe. By 1691 when the Treaty of Limerick closed the curtain on Jacobite rebellion in Ireland, they were joined by 'Wild Geese' mercenaries. This wealthy diaspora, with its network of Irish colleges, brigades and merchants, created an Irish Catholic nation-in-waiting on the European mainland. Ireland's less fortunate outcasts, however, were condemned to a grimmer fate. In the wake of Cromwell's reign of terror (1649-50), many were banished to the sun-baked plantations of the West Indies and a life of slavery or indentured service.

Throughout the 1700s, Irish scholars, soldiers, medics and artisans were plying their trades throughout Western Europe. The Irish community in Paris had made such an impact on the life of the city that the philosopher Montesquieu remarked: 'We have seen an entire nation driven from their native land, crossing the seas to settle in France, taking nothing with them to meet the bare necessities of life, except a formidable talent for argument.' While these exiles left few musical traces of their wanderings, their countrymen who settled in America bestowed an abundance of music on their new homeland.

THE SCOTS-IRISH IN THE APPALACHIANS

In the period 1690-1715 over 50,000 Presbyterians fled bad harvests, religious strife and rising rents in the Lowlands of Scotland and settled in northeast Ulster. By 1717-20 the generous leases which had attracted this influx of settlers began to expire. As old leases terminated, small farms were consolidated into larger tracts of prime land. Rents doubled in some parts of the province as land-hungry graziers outbid Presbyterian tenants for holdings. This rent war coincided with a period of religious persecution as well as a series of natural calamities – crop failures, bad weather and smallpox epidemics. Frustrated by their lot, thousands of Scots-Irish left for North America where they could escape discrimination from the established church and avoid

British mercantile constraints on their livelihoods – 200,000 of them left Ulster in the period 1700-1776.

Unlike their southern counterparts who would flee the Great Famine a century later, these Presbyterian emigrants settled in rural environments similar to those they had left behind in Ulster. Populating a vast area from the Ozarks to the Adirondacks, their influence was felt most in the Appalachian frontiers of the Carolinas, Virginia and Pennsylvania. During the early years of American independence, they contributed their talents to the birth of the new nation. Presidents Andrew Jackson and James Buchanan were first generation Scots-Irish.

These ambiguously termed 'Scots-Irish' dissenters transplanted whole communal networks to their new 'Land of Libertie'. Music, song and dance formed an essential part of their frontier milieu. They played music for flax-scutching frolics, weddings and other 'cayley' gatherings. Their music eventually evolved into Appalachian old-time music, and went on to influence country music, rock'n'roll and bluegrass. Appalachian hoedowns and square dances are a blend of steps and figures imported by Scots-Irish settlers in the 1700s, while clogging has cognates in the *sean nós* steps of Connemara and the Highland step dancing of Cape Breton Island in Atlantic Canada.

Scots-Irish tunes like 'Sally Gooden' and 'Turkey in the Straw' (popularised in the 1840s by Dan Emmet the black-and-white minstrel whose parents left Co Antrim to settle in Charles County, Maryland) have left an indelible imprint on early country and string-band recordings. Similarly, hybrid ballads like 'The Devil and the Farmer's Wife' (known in Ireland as 'The Women are Worse than the Men') and 'Down in the Willow Garden' (also known as 'Rose Connolly') reveal a remarkable fusion of Scottish, Irish and English traditions in the pioneer culture of the Appalachians. Dance tunes like 'Hop Light, Ladies' and

'Did You Ever See the Devil, Uncle Joe?' ('Miss McLeod's Reel') as well as the lesser-known 'Leather Breeches' ('Lord Mac Donald's Reel') have sustained those old traditions down to the present day in West Virginia, Kentucky, Pennsylvania and Tennessee.

IRISH MUSIC IN NEWFOUNDLAND

While the Scots-Irish chose the Appalachians as their place of voluntary exile, their contemporaries along the south coast opted for seasonal work in Newfoundland. By the mid 1700s, Waterford was one of the last ports of call for West Country fleets fishing for cod in Newfoundland's Grand Banks. As well as taking on final provisions for the crossing, the fleets recruited seasonal labourers from Waterford and its hinterlands in Cork, Tipperary and Wexford. Fishery workers signed on for two summers, which involved staying one winter in the brutal cold of Newfoundland, hence the term 'wintermen' by which they were known when they returned to port. By 1776, the traffic of Catholic migrants from Waterford to Newfoundland attracted the attention of the English traveller Arthur Young, who estimated that 5,000 of them sailed from the city annually.

Some wintermen chose to settle permanently in Newfoundland. By 1784 they comprised seven-eights of the population of St John's, which was named after St John's parish in Waterford city. Others established 'outport' communities along the island's Southern Shore from the Avalon Peninsula to Fogo Island. These communities, which were generally accessible by boat, were settled initially by Irish-speaking wintermen from Waterford, East Cork and Tipperary. Irish became so widespread by the 1780s that outport communities were requesting Irish-speaking priests from Ireland. They called their new home *Talamh an Éisc,* 'Land of the Fish', and endowed it with a rich repository of Irish traditional music, song and dance.

One of the most celebrated figures to emigrate to *Talamh an Éisc* in the 1740s was the indomitable Donncha Rua Mac Con Mara. Born in Cratloe, Co Clare, in 1715, Mac Con Mara was educated for the priesthood in Rome but was expelled for his 'wildness'. He returned to Ireland and found work as a schoolmaster in Waterford in 1740. His nostalgic poems *'Eachtra Giolla an Amaráin'*, ('The Adventures of a Luckless Fellow') and *'Bán Chnuic Éireann Ó'* ('The Fair Hills of Ireland') were probably written during his sojourn in Newfoundland from 1745-1756. The latter, which is still a popular song in Irish, voices the woes of the outport emigrant.

> Bíonn barr bog slím ar chaoin-chnuic Éireann
> Bán-chnuic Éireann Ó!
> 'S is fearr ná'n tír seo díogha gach sléibh' ann,
> Bán-chnuic Éireann Ó!
> Tá grá im chroí im inntinn féin,
> Bán-chnuic Éireann Ó!

James Clarence Mangan's translation captures the poet's sentiments of exile and loneliness:

> *The soil is rich and soft, the air is mild and bland*
> *O the fair hills of Éire Ó!*
> *Her barest rock is greener to me than this rude land*
> *O the fair hills of Éire Ó!*
> *O! in heart and soul, I shall ever love,*
> *The fair hills of Éire Ó!*

Two centuries after the settlement of wintermen in Newfoundland, the island still boasts a sizeable Irish population – complete with Waterford surnames like Power and Walsh, and pronounced Waterford accents which have defied the melting pot of time. Lancer sets are still danced in the outport communities along the island's Southern Shore where, until recently, mummers hunted the wren on St Stephen's Day, continuing an ancient tradition their predecessors brought from Ireland. An extensive collection of Irish ballads is housed today in the archives of the Memorial University of Newfoundland in St John's – a testament to the oral tradition of singers like Laurence Foley from Fogo Island and John Joe English from Branch, an outport community near Cape St Mary's. Likewise, the archaic whistle playing of Patsy Judge from Placentia Bay has encouraged Newfoundland's young musicians such as The Irish Descendants, to retrace the source of their music to the jigs and polkas, political ballads and maritime songs of the south of Ireland.

AUSTRALIA AND VAN DIEMEN'S LAND

In contrast to their countrymen who chose freely between a life of poverty in Ireland or a new beginning across the Atlantic, the Irish who sailed for Australia from 1793 onwards arrived in the British equivalent of a Siberian *gulag*. With the exception of a few land speculators, often the non-inheriting offspring of the Ascendancy, Irish deportees banished 'down under' during the next half-century included 30,000 men and 9,000 women sentenced to 'transportation for crimes against the crown'. Over twenty percent of them were political dissidents.

Some 'seditious United Irishmen' and Defenders were sent to Australia during the 1790s. However, the influx of 'Irish croppies' began in earnest after the failed rebellion of 1798, when their alliance with France crumbled against the forces of Cornwallis. They were joined later by 1,200 land-and-tithe protesters and other dissidents from societies like the Caravats, Whiteboys, Hearts of Steel and Ribbon Men, who were deported to New South Wales between 1815 and 1840. Irish prisoners in Australia were treated as a special class of Jacobin criminal, dangerous both ideologically and physically, and deserving of the most severe punishments for their treachery. In this stark reality of colonial incarceration, the Irish went on to form Australia's first white minority. It was hardly surprising that their plight should find a niche in the music and song of the period.

One of the most celebrated *sean nós* songs in the Déise Gaeltacht community of Co Waterford is the agrarian ballad *'Na Connerys'* It commemorates the three Connery brothers, Patrick, James and John, all of whom were transported to New South Wales between 1835 and 1838 after a series of land-related injustices. The brothers were natives of Bohadoon, a *clachán* community in the foothills of the Comeraghs. Much of this region, which comprised of poor marginal land, was forceably privatised by Ascendancy land agents (middlemen) in the early decades of the nineteenth century.

The Connery's tragic saga involved murder, land grabbing, daring prison breaks and eventual transportation as common criminals. Their trial at the Waterford Summer Assizes on 22 July 1835 attracted the attention of Alexis de Tocqueville and Gustave de Beaumont, who were travelling in Ireland at the time. In his critique of Irish social life, published four years afterwards, de Beaumont claimed that 'the peasant must possess a plot of ground, or starve. This is the secret of that extraordinary rivalry of which land is the object in Ireland. The condition of the unfortunate who has failed in attaining this object is lamentable; for unless he yields himself to starvation, he must either beg or rob.' The plight of the Connerys had a major impact on Co Waterford in the 1830s – in the garrison towns, as well as in the communal world of the *clachán* which they failed to defend. Among their Gaelic-speaking neighbours in Sliabh gCua (the area bounded by the Comeraghs, Galtees and Knockmealdown Mountains), the Connerys were considered *sárfhir,* 'great men', exemplary role models defending their people against the duplicity of the oppressor. Their heroic stature continues in the folk memory of the region today. This verse from the repertoire of Déise singer Nioclás Tóibín leaves us in little doubt:

> *A Chromthain mhallaithe gúimse deacair ort a's gráin Mhic Dé,*
> *A's ar an ngasra úd 'tá ceangailte go dlúth led' thaobh,*
> *Mar sibh do dhearbhaigh i láthair Choisdealaigh ar 'n triúr fear séimh*
> *'S a chuir na Connerys thar na fairgí 'dtí's na New South Wales.*

> Oh cursed Crotty, I wish misery to you and the wrath of the Lord
> As well as your associate who stood firmly by your side
> It was ye who produced the evidence for Crossley against three fine men
> That sent the Connerys over the seas to New South Wales.

Irish convicts who defied the system and became bushrangers in Australia were also eulogised in song. The earliest of these 'outback' Robin Hoods was Dubliner Jack Donoghue (1806-1830) who was transported to Australia in 1825. His dashing exploits and defiance of Governor Darling are recounted in the eponymous song 'Bold Jack Donoghue' which earned him a legendary role in Australian folk history. His example was followed by Jim Doolan 'The Wild Colonial Boy', and later on by Ned Kelly – all of whom represent an Irish counter-culture outside the official mainframe of colonial history in Australia. Just as the jail journals of the Young Irelanders and the Fenian ballads in the 1870s reinforced the *gulag* image of Van Diemen's Land (Tasmania), the repertoire of the 'bush band' a century afterwards underlines the contribution of Irish felons to the folk music of modern Australia.

IRISH TRADITIONAL MUSIC IN SCOTLAND

Cultural exchange between Highland Scotland and Ireland had been buttressed over the centuries by a common Gaelic language and maintained by bardic poets who were shared by patrons on both sides of the North Channel. Despite the moral constraints of the Scottish reformation and the sectarian tension of the Ulster plantation, travelling bards, dancing masters and musicians continued to ply their crafts between Ireland and Scotland in the seventeenth and eighteenth centuries. They served the needs of an extended Gaelic world which survived on the periphery of political and religious upheaval.

Remnants of this world are still evident today in the jigs, reels and step dances which are common to both Ireland and Cape Breton Island in Canada. Populated by Gaelic-speaking Scottish and Irish communities after the Highland clearances (1770s-1820s), the island houses a vibrant corpus of music, which predates the narrative folk music and regimental piping of nineteenth-century Scotland. London's exercise in 'internal colonialism' clearly failed to curb the creative vigour of these Gaelic communities – even in exile.

A huge repertoire of airs and dance tunes serve to index the centuries of exchange between Ireland and Scotland. As early as the eighteenth century the Munster poets borrowed airs like 'Scots over the Water to Charlie' which was also known as *Seán Buí*. Other early borrowings include 'The White Cockade', 'The Cuckoo's Nest' and 'The Boyne Water' to which the Munster poet Piaras Mac Gearailt composed *Rosc Catha na Mumhan*. By the end of the eighteenth century traditional musicians in Ireland and Scotland shared an abundant crop of reels, many attributed to known Scottish composers. 'Bonnie Kate' for example (popularised by the fiddling of Michael Coleman), was first published as 'The Bonnie Lass of Fisherrow' around 1760. It was composed by Daniel Dow, a fiddle player from Perthshire. The compositions of William Marshall were also popular among Irish musicians, especially 'The Duke of Gordon's Rant' which was known in Ireland as 'Lord Gordon's Reel'. Miss Stirling's 'The Perthshire Hunt' also found its way to Ireland, where it acquired about forty Irish titles including 'The Boyne Hunt'. The well-known tune 'The Fairy Reel', is also of Scottish origin. It was composed by Neil Gow for the Fife Hunt Ball in 1802. It became such a favourite in Ireland that a special dance *'Cor na Síoga'* was composed for it. Popular reels like 'Lord MacDonald', 'Miss McLeod' (and its jig variant 'The Campbells are Coming'), 'Rakish Paddy', 'The Flogging Reel' and 'Lucy Campbell' are all clearly Scottish in origin.

PROFILE: RORY 'DALL' Ó CATHÁIN (*c*1550-*c*1640)

Rory 'Dall' Ó Catháin was born in Co Derry into a wealthy Gaelic family. Much of what we know of him is contained in the memoirs of the harper Arthur O'Neill (1737-1816) which were transcribed at the Belfast Harp Festival in 1792. According to O'Neill, Rory 'Dall' (or Blind Rory) inherited extensive holdings in Coleraine, Garvagh and Newtown-Limavaddy, Co Derry. Before receiving his inheritance, he was given the title *Oireachtaidhe Ó Catháin* (Chief Ó Catháin) by the O'Neills of Tyrone.

Despite his wealth and political standing, Rory Dall chose to learn the harp and became a travelling performer, albeit with a supporting retinue of servants as befitted an Irish lord. Much of Ó Catháin's life was spent travelling in Scotland, where he composed several harp tunes for members of the Scottish aristocracy. They include 'Port Gordon', composed for the Countess of Gordon, and 'Port Athol' for the Countess of Athol. One of his tunes, 'Rory Dall's Port', provided the music for Robert Burns's well-known love song 'Ae fond kiss, and then we sever!'

Several accounts of Ó Catháin's travels in Scotland have survived, not least the visit he made to the home of Lady Eglinton. Unaware of his political status, she arrogantly demanded a tune. Her lack of respect offended him and he left her house angry. On realising her misdemeanor, she quickly sought reconciliation. Her apology impressed him enough to merit a tune entitled *'Da Mihi Manum – Tabhair dom do Lámh'* (Give Me Your Hand), which has survived down to the present day and still enjoys widespread popularity among Irish and Scottish musicians. This tune won him widespread acclaim all over Scotland. It even reached the ears of James I of England who accorded him an audience. According to Arthur O'Neill's memoirs, Ó Catháin was not at all impressed by the king's condescending style. When the surly Stuart laid his hand on Ó Catháin's shoulder, as a token of authority, the harper announced that 'a greater man than ever James was laid his hand on my shoulder.' 'Who is that?' asked the king abruptly. 'O'Neill, my liege,' replied Ó Catháin, standing up to defy his astonished detractor.

PIPERS, SPAILPÍNS AND PATRIOTS: PRE-FAMINE IRELAND

The 1790s was a pivotal decade in Irish political and cultural history. The period witnessed the birth of modern Irish nationalism, set in motion by Wolfe Tone, the United Irishmen and the Rising of 1798. It also saw the emergence of an antiquarian and cultural revival among the middle classes which had a direct impact on Irish traditional music. Just as the political climate was influenced by the Enlightenment, as well as the revolutions in America and France, the cultural climate was inspired by the Romantic movement which was sweeping across Europe. The first Celtic Revival in the 1790s set out to explore the 'authentic' Irish past and the living traditions of its Gaelic-speaking peasantry. It found eager advocates in Charlotte Brooke, whose *Reliques of Irish Poetry* was published in 1789, and Edward Bunting, whose *General Collection of the Ancient Music of Ireland* appeared in 1796.

THE BELFAST HARPERS' FESTIVAL

Three music types survived in Ireland down to the middle of the eighteenth century. Each can be identified with the main cultural groupings at the time – the atrophying harp music of the Gaelic aristocracy, the European art music of the Protestant Ascendancy and the vibrant dance music of the Gaelic-speaking peasantry. As noted above, by the end of the century a serious attempt was being made to resuscitate the orally transmitted harp music of Gaelic Ireland. This cultural venture coincided with the earliest attempts to formulate a doctrine of republicanism in Ireland. It also ran parallel with the revival of interest in folk music on the European mainland. As plans for the Belfast Harpers' Festival were being laid, the Society of United Irishmen was being formed by Wolfe Tone, Thomas Russell and Henry Joy McCracken. Both Russell and McCracken were involved in organising the Harpers' Festival with Dr James MacDonnell, a leading Belfast citizen who wanted 'to preserve from oblivion the few fragments that have been permitted to remain' of the country's harp music.

The Belfast Harpers' Festival took place in the city's Exchange Rooms on 11-13 July 1792, in the midst of celebrations commemorating the Fall of the Bastille three years previously. In all, ten exponents, including one woman, answered MacDonnell's call. The oldest harper to attend was the blind nonagenarian Dennis Hempson (1697-1807) who contributed *'An Chuilfhionn'*, ('The Coolin'), among other harp compositions to the assembly. He was the only performer to play in the traditional Irish manner with long fingernails on strings of brass.

The music played at the Belfast Festival was transcribed by nineteen-year-old Edward Bunting, who had been appointed substitute organist at a Belfast parish church at the sprightly age of eleven. Bunting was born in Armagh in 1773 to an Irish mother and an English father. The nineteen-year-old was cautioned by Dr MacDonnell to take down the various airs played by the visiting harpers 'without adding a single note to the old melodies'. Hence he began his first celebrated collection, which was to be followed by two more before his death in 1843. However, despite the word of caution from the good doctor, Bunting's work was transcribed for ears that were more acquainted with the music of Handel and Mozart than the harp compositions of Gaelic Ireland.

After travelling to Tyrone, Derry and parts of north Connacht to complete his collection, Bunting published his *General Collection of the Ancient Music of Ireland* in 1796. His Dublin-based contemporary Thomas Moore mined it as an immediate treasury for his own drawing-room compositions. A shrewd venture in musical antiquarianism, Moore's *Irish Melodies* first appeared in 1808 and contained sixteen airs, eleven of which had been lifted directly from Bunting's work. Nine more serialised volumes of Moore's melodies, containing his own Regency lyrics set to music, were published up to 1834. While many of his lucrative compositions were culled from traditional melodies, Moore himself claimed that his drawing-room songs, with their stage-Irish *mavourneens* and *acushlas*, were composed for the pianofortes of the rich and educated. Aggrieved by Moore's failure to acknowledge him publicly, Bunting foolishly tried to compete with him. In 1809, he published his second *General Collection of the Ancient Music of Ireland*, which contained twenty songs written by Thomas Campbell and other lesser-known scribes. His final collection *Ancient Music of Ireland* was published in 1840 and was dedicated to Queen Victoria.

THE UILLEANN PIPES REACH MATURITY

The industrial revolution, coupled with the creative synergy of the Romantic period, resulted in the invention of several new musical instruments in Europe, among them the free-reed accordion and concertina. In Ireland, native pipe-makers were refining their skills to perfect one of the world's most distinctive multi-reed instruments. As Edward Bunting hurried to salvage the last of the native harp music in the 1790s, the *uilleann* or union pipes reached their present state of development, combining drones, chanter and regulators to create what some commentators called the 'Irish organ'. (The term 'union' refers to the union of regulators with the chanter, not the Act of Union of 1801.) Published music and tutors for the pipes followed shortly afterwards. The first and most prominent publication was O'Farrell's *Collection of National Irish Music for the Union Pipes,* which appeared in London around 1800. O'Farrell, a piper from Clonmel who had settled in London, also included a treatise 'with the most perfect instruction ever yet published' for the pipes. His *Pocket Companion for the Irish or Union Pipes* followed in 1810. Like the first collection, it contained airs and dance tunes, many of which had never been published before. It included the earliest known version of 'The Fox Chase', which has since become a *pièce de résistance* for pipers.

In filling the void left by the demise of the harper, the piper now became the keeper of slow airs, clan marches and what have come to be known generically as 'piping pieces'. Like the harper before him, he enjoyed superior status to other traditional musicians. This mantle of prestige was based to some extent on a pompous self-image inherited from the native harpers. In 1839 the collector George Petrie remarked that the piper Patrick Connelly, one of his principal sources of music in Galway, lived in 'tolerably comfortable circumstances'. Connelly, it seems, had a high opinion of his own music, and a strong feeling of 'decent pride' He played only for strong farmers and gentry, and would not lower his dignity by playing in a tap room. Blind from infancy, yet mindful of his superior status, he would perform for 'commoners' only on rare occasions.

MUSIC AND POLITICS: 1798-1843

Just as American defiance of British rule in the 1770s influenced the Ascendancy Ireland of Henry Grattan, so the French Revolution, with its novel ideas of liberty, equality and fraternity, influenced the radical Ireland of Wolfe Tone two decades later. The Society of United Irishmen which Tone founded in 1791 set out to unite Catholics, Protestants and Presbyterian Dissenters and press for radical reforms. However, England's war with republican France led to severe military repression in Ireland. The United Irishmen eventually decided to launch a rebellion in 1798. Despite help from France, the rebellion was disorganised and was quickly suppressed. Instead of breaking Ireland's link with England, the 1790s saw that link strengthened as never before. After the defeat of 1798, the London government decided to unite the British and Irish parliaments. When the Act of Union became law in 1801, Ireland ceased to have a parliament of its own. Irish MPs now attended parliament in Westminster, where they represented an Ascendancy minority.

Some of these events attracted the attention of musicians, while others failed to make any impact on folk repertoires. One of the popular hornpipes of the period, 'The Rights of Man', was possibly inspired by Tom Paine's political tome. Contemporary reports confirm that Paine was read widely in Belfast in the 1790s. In contrast to the Jacobite rising of the 1740s, the rebellion of 1798 failed to attract a widespread response from Irish language scribes. The most notable exception was the Cork poet Mícheál

Óg Ó Longáin, who wrote '*Buachaillí Loch Garmain*'. Ó Longáin was a member of the United Irishmen and a strong advocate of republican ideas. His son Peadar later penned the celebrated '98 song '*Sliabh na mBan*', which still enjoys considerable popularity among *sean nós* singers.

Songs in English present a different picture. Authentic '98 ballads include 'The Croppy Boy', 'Billy Byrne of Ballymanus', '*Cearbhall Bán Mo Chroí*', '*The Shan Van Vocht*' and '*Roddy McCorley*', all of which became popular shortly after the rebellion. The heroics and tragedy of '98 continued to inspire English language ballads well into the following century. 'The Grave of Wolfe Tone' was composed by Thomas Davis and a new version of 'The Croppy Boy' appeared in *The Nation* in 1845. A half century later, PJ McCall (1861-1919) wrote 'Boolavogue' (also known as 'Fr Murphy') to coincide with the centenary of the rising in 1898.

While the rebellions in Wexford and Antrim were recorded in song, the politics of war-torn France in the early 1800s captured the mercurial imaginations of Irish musicians. Napoleon Bonaparte, for example, enjoys a significant presence in Irish music. Not alone does his musical code name, 'The Green Linnet', occur frequently in contemporary songs, but his exploits were used to title a suite of tunes and set dances throughout the nineteenth century. These include well-known dance pieces like 'Napoleon Crossing the Rhine', 'The Downfall of Paris', 'Madame Bonaparte' and 'The Salamanca Reel'.

With the exception of Robert Emmet's attempt to seize Dublin Castle in 1803, most attempts to reform Ireland's inequalities in the early 1800s came from within the parliamentary process. In 1823 a Catholic barrister, Daniel O'Connell, founded the Catholic Association to campaign for political liberty for Irish Catholics. This campaign was quickly converted into a mass movement. Its success eventually forced Westminster to grant Catholic Emancipation in 1829. Riding on a tide of political success, O'Connell now pushed for repeal of the Union. Addressing monster meetings and rallying parliament for repeal, O'Connell became the most popular public figure in Ireland. As well as being lauded by the press, The Liberator, as O'Connell was dubbed, became a cherished icon of folk poets, musicians and singers throughout rural Ireland. He is remembered in tunes like 'O'Connell's Farewell to Dublin', 'The Repeal of the Union' and the farcical ballad 'Babies by Steam', which hints guilefully at O'Connell's 'paternal' prowess.

TOURISTS AND MUSICIANS IN THE EARLY 1800s

While cosmopolitan intellectuals were absorbing the novels of Dickens and Balzac and the Romantic compositions of Liszt and Chopin, their wealthier contemporaries were cultivating a taste for exotic tourism. With the construction of canals and vast road improvements in the first half of the nineteenth century, the West of Ireland, like the Highlands of Scotland, became a picturesque mecca for upper-class tourists and evangelists. Travellers from England and mainland Europe left a mosaic of commentary on the state of Irish music. Mr and Mrs Samuel Carter Hall left a rather 'sobering' account of the difficulties facing uilleann pipers during Fr Matthew's temperance crusade of the 1830s. They praised the Temperance Society's brass bands and recommended the building of assembly rooms and the circulation of books to educate 'the victims of whiskey'. They hoped that brass bands would increase, 'for the wonderful change that has been wrought in the habits of the people has unquestionably driven the piper and the fiddler out of fashion. Indeed, it is absolutely necessary that some healthful excitement should be introduced to replace the unhealthy excitement formerly induced by whiskey,' and, presumably, by thirst-inducing music.

In contrast to the chiding observations of the Halls, Capo de Feuillide's view of the traditional musician is much more discerning. A journalist and critic writing at the height of the Romantic Movement in France, de Feuillide travelled throughout Ireland in 1837. His two volume *l'Irlande* was published in 1839. He remarked that an implicit indifference towards the Irish language characterised much of the nationalist movement in pre-famine Ireland. Mindful of the complex cultural tensions between Irish-speaking rural communities and their colonial rulers, de Feuillide is critical of Thomas Moore's usurpation of songs in the Irish language. He noted that *'quant au peuple, il ne sait pas ce que c'est que Thomas Moore'* ('as far as the people are concerned, they know nothing of Thomas Moore'). He laments the passing of the harp which had ceded its place to the piano in the drawing rooms of the Ascendancy and, in the thatched houses of *le peuple,* to the uilleann pipes. Spending much of his time with Irish-speaking communities in Connemara, de Feuillide noted the words of songs phonetically, which he had dictated to him by his hosts, and excused himself for not being able to transcribe their melodies.

MUSIC IN THE RURAL *CLACHÁN*

On the eve of the Great Famine, social organisation in the isolated uplands, blanket bogs and shoreline areas of the West of Ireland was determined by the rural *clachán*. This was a nucleated cluster of farmhouses, where holdings were organised communally, and families were connected through close kinship ties. Life within these communities was characterised by a precarious potato diet, lazy-bed cultivation and a scattering of Rundale plots (long strips of open farmland) which allowed land of varying quality to be shared by the community on an egalitarian basis. These *clacháns* housed nearly three quarters of the population of Ireland prior to the famine.

Occasions of music-making in these communities followed the cyclical calendar of the agricultural year. *Imbolg* (St Bridget's Day), *Bealtine* (May Day), *Lughnasa* (festival of Lugh in late July to early August, also known as (Mountain or Garland Sunday) and *Samhain* (Halloween) were the main festive days and sowing, harvesting and potato-digging were planned around them. The completion of work on the land was celebrated with music and dancing as the *meitheal* (communal workforce) of neighbours and kin congregated in *clachán* kitchens. Sometimes these festivities coincided with race meetings, fairs and hurling matches. The patron days of saints were also celebrated by *clachán* communities. The collector Francis O'Neill recalled that a piper usually played for dancers in the 'refreshment' tents, where 'repentant' customers gathered once they had completed their 'rounds' at the blessed well of the local patron saint.

Wakes and weddings were invariably occasions for music. While wakes were the preserve of the *mná caoine* (keeners), weddings attracted a full complement of musicians and dancers, with pride of place going to the piper. In his *Fairy Legends and Traditions of the South of Ireland* (1825-8), Thomas Crofton Croker noted that the best room at the wedding was reserved for the bride and bridegroom, the priest, the piper, and 'respectable' guests from among the neighbouring gentry. After the wedding, two collections were taken up, one for the priest and the other for the piper. Itinerant pipers enjoyed considerable status in western townlands. They were carriers of news as well as entertainment, and their arrival generally prompted a *ragairne* (house dance). They often followed established itineraries which were built around the work year of their patrons. Walking distance was a critical factor in plotting out a comfortable circuit, especially for blind pipers who usually travelled with a child to guide them from place to place.

SONGWRITERS ON THE EVE OF THE FAMINE

The music collections made in the decades prior to the famine confirm that love songs like *'Dónall Óg', 'Úna Bhán'* and *'Saileog Ruadh'* were especially popular among Irish-speaking communities in the West of Ireland. All moods and emotions are expressed in these songs, from the simple delight of courtship, to the poignant resignation of unrequited love. Ironically, patriotic songs like *'Cáit Ní Dhuibhir', 'Róisín Dubh'* and *'An Druimín Donn Dílis'* were scarce in Irish. The remaining store of Irish songs comprised of work songs, religious songs, laments, satires, as well as lullabies and children's recreational songs. Among the most popular genre of pre-famine songs were songs of the supernatural. Fairylore was particularly popular in Irish-speaking communities. Their songs recounted ominous tales of abductions, changelings and musical exchanges with the fairies.

Folk poets enjoyed a privileged position in Irish-speaking communities. Two of the most prominent folk poets during the pre-famine decades were Antoine Ó Reachtabhra (*c*1783-1835) and Tomás Rua Ó Súilleabháin (1785-1848). Ó Reachtabhra was born in Co Mayo and spent most of his life travelling the roads of Galway and Mayo as an itinerant fiddler. He composed poetry for people as poor as himself, and his verses live on in songs like *'Anach Cuain'* and *'Cill Aodáin'*. Douglas Hyde later edited his poems in the collection *Abhráin atá Leagtha ar an Reachtúire,* published in Dublin in 1903. Like Ó Reachtabhra, Tomás Rua was a fiddler. He also worked as a hedge schoolmaster on the Iveragh peninsula in west Kerry. He was one of the first poets to extol the greatness of Daniel O'Connell, whom he saw as an heir to the Jacobite cause. His most celebrated song was *'Amhrán na Leabhar',* ('Song of the Books'), which recounts the tragic loss of his books during a boating accident on the crossing between Caherdaniel and Portmagee. The poem gives a rare insight into the texts used by the hedge schoolmaster – Euclid, Cato, the New Testament, the *Psalter of Cashel* and Keating's *History of Ireland*. The songs of Tomás Rua were published in Dublin in 1914 by Séamus Dubh Ó Fiannachta as *Amhráin Thomáis Ruaidh: The Songs of Tomás Rua O'Sullivan the Iveragh Poet*.

The spread of the English language during the early 1800s was causing a loss of traditional songs in Irish. This was further accelerated by the National School system introduced by Stanley's Primary Education Bill in 1831. Songs in English, as well as bilingual *macaronic* songs, began to supplant Irish language songs. English and Lowland Scottish songs, as well as Anglo-Irish songs, enjoyed considerable popularity on the eve of the famine. Ballads were dispersed through ballad sheets printed initially in England and circulated in Dublin and other towns along the east coast. Songs which reached pre-famine audiences in this way include 'Lord Baker', 'Captain Wedderburn's Courtship' and 'Barbara Allen'. Anglo-Irish folk songs were songs composed by Irish people whose mother tongue was now English. The ballads of the Young Irelanders, which appeared in *The Nation* from 1842 onwards, fall into this latter category.

On the eve of the famine, the *London Times* described the songs and poems of the Young Irelanders as being far more dangerous than the speeches of O'Connell. Nonetheless, their popular publications reflect a booming era in ballad composition. Charles Gavin Duffy's *Ballad Poetry of Ireland* appeared in 1845, after which Thomas Davis wanted to create a ballad history of Ireland. Edward Walsh's *Irish Popular Songs with English Metrical Translations* was published in 1847 and James Clarence Mangan and John O'Daly's *Poets and Poetry of Munster* followed in 1849. While several other ballad collections appeared in the 1840s, few could contend with James

Hardiman's *Irish Minstrelsy* which was published in London in 1831. Relying to some degree on the work of Bunting and O'Conor of Stowe, Hardiman's comprehensive collection consists of four parts – the compositions of O'Carolan; sentimental songs; Jacobite relics; and a closing section entitled 'Odes and Elegies'. Unlike his romantic predecessors, Hardiman presents a pragmatic reappraisal of Jacobite Ireland. In his work, the anti-English *aisling* of Penal times is reproduced in full, and the 'hidden Ireland' of the period is allowed to reach the ears of the Irish public for the first time.

LAMENT FOR THE SPAILPÍN

Of all the social classes in pre-famine Ireland, few have received the same attention from the musician as the *spailpín*, or landless labourer. According to the Devon Commission of 1843, farm workers could be divided into three categories – the unmarried servant living with his employer; the married labourer holding his own cabin and a small plot of land from a farmer at a fixed rent; and the *spailpín* or landless labourer, holding nothing other than a cabin. Obliged to hawk his labour wherever he found work, the *spailpín* survived on a system of conacre in the hope of growing enough crops to pay his rent and keep food on his table. Earning as little as eight pence to a shilling a day, the commissioners declared that the *spailpín* belonged to the most 'wretched of the many wretched classes in Ireland'. To supplement the taking of conacre in times of crisis, the *spailpín* became a temporary migrant worker. This was particularly common among mountainous and bogland communities in the West of Ireland, from where the *spailpín* was dispatched to find work along the rich pastures of the Shannon and the fertile plains of Munster and Leinster. The scorned ritual of lining up to be measured at the hiring fair is well attested in the songs of the *spailpín*. Little had changed since the eighteenth-century Kerry poet described the contempt with which he was treated by the strong farmers of Tipperary in 'An Spailpín Fánach':

> *Go deo deo arís ní raghad go Caiseal*
> *Ag díol ná ag reic mo shláinte,*
> *Ná ar mhargadh na saoirse in shuí cois balla*
> *I'm scaoinse ar leaththaoibh sráide -*
> *Bodairí na tíre ag tíocht ar a gcapall*
> *Dá fhiafraí an bhfuilim hirálta.*
> *O! Téanam chun siúil, tá an cúrsa fada;*
> *Seo ar siúl an spailpín fánach.*

> I'll never again go to Cashel
> Selling and bartering my health,
> Nor at hiring fair sit down against a wall
> Nor hang about the street –
> The boors of the district coming on their horses
> Asking if I'm hired.
> O! Let's make a start, the journey is long
> It's off with the wandering labourer.

The *spailpín*, who was the primary victim of the Great Famine, is also remembered in airs like 'Caoineadh an Spailpín', ('Lament for the Spailpín'), and the song 'A Spailpín, A Rúin' as well as the Connemara song 'Peigín is Peadar', a versified form of a prose folk tale recounting the adventures of a *spailpín* who returned to his family after spending twenty-one years in service.

If the *spailpín* received his share of posterity from the song-writer, so too did his main staple, the potato, which was introduced to Ireland by Walter Raleigh. Originating in the Andean Highlands of South America, it created agronomic conditions in Ireland in which a landless cottier class could survive with no capital other than a spade and *ciseán* (basket) of seed potatoes. In the half-century before the Great Famine, this class proliferated at an unprecedented rate, despite its location at twenty degrees latitude further north of the equator than any other class of its kind. The musician and the dancer each found time to celebrate the potato and the rituals associated with its cultivation. '*Maide na bPlanndaí*' – ('The Planting Stick'), a solo pantomime imitating the tilling, planting and digging of the potato – was danced to the air of the jig 'Bryan O'Lynn'. Singers too paid homage to the potato:

> *Ba iad ár gcaraid iad ó am ár gcliabháin*
> *Ach is é mo dhiobháil iad imeacht uainn*
> *Ba mhaith an chuidheacht iad is an t-údar rince*
> *Bhíodh spóirt is siamsa againn in aice leo.*

> They were our friends from the cradle
> Their going from us is to my deprivation
> They were good company and a source of dancing
> We had fun and entertainment beside them.

SET DANCING IN THE PRE-FAMINE ERA

Quadrilles were introduced into Ireland by soldiers returning from the Napoleonic Wars. Evolving into traditional set dancing, their popularity reached its height between the end of the Napoleonic Wars and the outbreak of the Great Famine in 1845. They were so popular that even the Knight of Glin in west Limerick gave orders that dancing masters within his domain were to teach these new dances as they were danced in France and Portugal. Various adaptations of quadrille figures developed during the 1830s and 1840s, the most prominent being the 'Lancers', the 'Plain Set' and the 'Caledonian', the latter of which was possibly introduced into west Clare by Scottish sappers who came to work there with the Ordnance Survey Commission in the 1830s. Other urban adaptations of the quadrille were the 'Orange and Green', the 'Paris Set' and the '*Televara*'.

SILENCE IN THE LAND OF SONG:
POST-FAMINE IRELAND

The potatoes that failed brought the nation to agony,
The poorhouse bare, and the dreadful coffin ship,
And in mountain graves do they in hundreds lie,
Hunger taken to their beds of clay.

Famine Ballad

The Napoleonic Wars precipitated a major growth in tillage farming in Ireland, the produce of which was used to feed the armies in Europe. When the war ended in 1815, the rural economy began to switch from tillage to pasture which was less labour-intensive and favoured large farms. This pragmatic change swelled the ranks of the landless and the unemployed, most of whom were dependent on the potato as a primary food crop. To complicate this reality, the rural population continued to expand during the following decades, particularly in the West of Ireland where Rundale farming and *clachán* settlements were the norm.

The 1841 census registered an Irish population of 8,175,124. The majority of these people lived below the subsistence line in western areas like Clare, which housed 300 people per square mile of arable land. The English statesman Disraeli declared that Ireland was the 'most populated country in Europe', with some regions on a par with China. As long as an adequate diet of potatoes lasted, such regional densities could subsist. However, one rupture in the food cycle would throw the whole system into disarray. This rupture came in the form of the potato blight *Phytophthora infestans,* a deadly parasitical fungus carried by wind. First identified in Flanders, it reached Ireland late in the summer of 1845 and thrived in the country's damp climate.

The Great Famine lasted until 1849 and rocked Irish society to its foundations. By 1851 the population had fallen drastically. Approximately 1.5 million people died of starvation and disease, while over a million others left the country. The Tory government under Robert Peel appointed a commission to examine the blight, but it had no immediate success. Peel then imported £100,000 worth of Indian corn to prevent food prices from rising. Relief committees and public works were organised to relieve distress and allow famine victims to buy food. Peel's emergency measures were administered by Charles Trevelyan who was most unsympathetic to the principle of government aid. Peel's Tory government was replaced by Russell's Whig government in 1846. From then on, *laissez faire* ideas prevailed and food purchases stopped. The winter of 1847, known as 'Black '47', was the worst of the famine winters, both in terms of severe weather conditions and human fatalities. Voluntary schemes were initiated by groups like the Quakers in an effort to relieve the distress of the hungry. Soup kitchens were set up, but thousands continued to perish as a result of disease (typhus and relapsing fever) and exposure to bad weather. Public works were eventually replaced by direct relief, but local Poor Law Unions, already stretched to extremes, could not bear the cost of this relief.

By the end of the 1840s, the Irish countryside had changed radically. New proprietors and land-hungry graziers had increased their dominions, while cottiers, *spailpíns* and bankrupt landlords had failed to rally through the crisis. At the same time, colonies of proselytisers vied with their Catholic adversaries for the souls of the survivors. Traditional musicians were also affected by the famine and its diaspora. Thousands died with the onslaught of starvation and disease, while others followed their audiences into exile in the New World. Folklore recalls pipers, fiddlers and dancing masters ending their days in the workhouse, and contemporary collectors of traditional music reflected sadly on the silence which had fallen on 'the land of song'. Evaluating the cultural cleansing of the famine, the music collector George Petrie wrote bleakly on the state of his informants in the 1850s. His despair is matched by an urgency to collect what remained of the music of Gaelic Ireland: 'The land of song was no longer tuneful; or, if a human sound met the traveller's ear, it was only that of the feeble and despairing wail for the dead. This awful unwonted silence struck more fearfully upon their imaginations.'

The cataclysm exacted a cruel toll from a once-thriving tradition of work songs. With a radical change in land use, small tillage plots gave way to large pasture lands. This decreased the demand for agricultural labour. Deprived of the activities that once validated them, traditional songs associated with ploughing, reaping and sowing, as well as their related domestic chores, declined and eventually disappeared from the oral tradition.

ANGUISH IN THE FOLK VERSES

Contemporary song-writers had their own unique insight into local conditions. They recalled the traumatic events of the famine in a way which was different from official histories of the period. Although few in number, the Irish-language songs of the famine era focus on the harsh realities of mortality, destitution and emigration, and seem closer to the immediate suffering of the victims. Describing the misfortune of his neighbours near Craughwell in east Galway, song-writer Peatsaí Ó Callanáin (1791-1865) recalls the widespread dependence on the potato in his requiem *'Na Fataí Bána'*, 'The White Potatoes'. The song focuses particularly on the autumn blight of 1846. Ó Callanáin reminds his listeners that the local poorhouse and the hospital are full of famine victims and adds that English public work schemes are totally ineffective in countering the hopelessness of the countryside.

Other famine songs like *'Soup House Mhuigh-Iorrais'*

('Moyrus Soup House'), *'Amhrán na bPrátaí Dubha'* ('Song of the Black Potatoes'), *'An Droch-Shaoghal'* ('The Bad Life') and *'Dúchan na bPrátaí'* ('The Rotting of the Potatoes') all reflect the same gruesome themes of hopelessness, disease and deprivation. Surprisingly few of them attribute blame to any external source and very few are explicitly aware of the roles being played by the political architects of the day, from Peel in the early years of the famine to Trevelyan and Lord John Russell in the latter years. Any ire which these Irish songs contain is directed mainly towards local landlords, bailiffs, corn dispensers, clerics (of both denominations) and Poor Law Guardians.

As well as indexing local fatalities, deprivation and poor law conditions, songs in Irish also lament the lack of the gaiety and courtship, music and matchmaking, which characterised their communities before the tragedy struck. A vivid folk recollection of famine conditions on the Dingle peninsula, *'Amhrán an Ghorta'*, offers this social insight:

> *Tá scamall éigin os cionn na hÉireann*
> *Nár fhan dúil i gcéilíocht ag fear ná ag mnaoi;*
> *Ní athníonn éinne des na daoine a chéile,*
> *Is tá an suan céanna ar gach uile ní.*
> *Ní miste spéirbhean bheith amuigh go déanach,*
> *Níor fhan aon tréine ins na fir a bhí,*
> *Níl ceol in aon áit ná suim ina dhéanamh,*
> *Is ní aithním glao cheart ag bean chun bídh.*

> There is some cloud over Ireland
> Men and women have no desire for courtship;
> The people do not recognise each other,
> And the same drowsiness has fallen on everything.
> An enchanted lady must now stay out late,
> There is no strength left in the men that were,
> There is no music any place nor a desire to make it,
> I hear no clear shout from a woman [to come] for food.

'THE LANDLORD AND THE SHERIFF CAME'

The Irish language was one of the principal victims of the Great Famine. Its decline, particularly in the West of Ireland, undermined much of the folklore, popular superstitions and folk beliefs that sustained the cultural geography of the music-maker. The new anglicised placenames of post-famine Ireland failed to connect with an older world of townlands, Rundale strips and 'walking' distances. Likewise, the *dinnsheanchas* (placename lore) associated with tunes, failed to translate into utilitarian English.

Songs in English offer a different perspective on the famine tragedy. Some were nationalist ballads which viewed the famine as a callous act of imperialism; others were songs of emigration which recalled the disaster in the midst of exile and loneliness. The appalling reality of overcrowded workhouses, cartloads of uncoffined bodies and quick-lime burials is evoked in the emigrant ballad 'Lone Shanakyle'. Composed in the United States by the Clare poet Thomas Madigan (1797-1881), the song is a requiem to the 3,900 people who died in the workhouse in Kilrush in the years 1847-1849. Most of these victims were buried coffinless in a mass grave in Shanakyle outside Kilrush on the lower Shannon.

> Sad, sad is my fate in this weary exile,
> Dark, dark is the night cloud o'er lone Shanakyle
> Where the murdered sleep silently, pile upon pile
> In the coffinless graves of poor Érin.

As economic pressure on landlords increased from 1847 onwards, mass evictions became the order of the day. A panic-induced cure for rental default, evictions added to the disparities of the countryside. Its inhuman horrors were mirrored in English-language ballads throughout the closing decades of the last century. Composed long after the events it recounts, the Cork ballad 'Skibbereen' epitomises the interwoven themes of famine, destitution and exile. Its graphic portrayal of eviction and its call for revenge helped to politicise the famine, particularly for Irish immigrants in America:

> It's well I do remember that bleak December day.
> When the landlord and the sheriff came to drive us all away,
> They set our roof on fire with their damning yellow spleen,
> And when it fell, the crash was heard all over Skibbereen.

FENIANS, THE LAND WAR AND HOME RULE

In the wake of the famine, life in rural Ireland became increasingly hard and materialistic as people became preoccupied with private property, ownership and inheritance. In this new economic ethos, the strong farmer came into his own, while the old world of the *clachán* with its gatherings of folk poets, dancing masters and travelling pipers was seen as lethargic and morally suspect. The synods of Thurles and Maynooth, convened in 1850 and 1875, initiated a new liturgical revolution in Catholic Ireland. The priest became a social as well as a moral arbiter, especially in country areas where entertainment was communal and unsupervised. Some priests scoured the countryside hunting for courting couples and purging fiddlers from crossroad dances. In conducting these crusades, they felt they were protecting their flocks from immoral past-times and sinful gatherings.

While Ireland's social life was being policed by a reformed clergy, its political life shifted from Fenian separatism in the 1860s, to land agitation and Home Rule in the following decades. All of these popular movements found a voice among the songsmiths and musicians of the day. Fenianism gave a new lease of life to the political ballads of Thomas Davis and the Young Irelanders. It also spawned its own crop of political songs like 'Down Erin's Lovely Lee', 'Come to the Bower' and 'The Fenian's

Escape', the latter a ballad about a daring escape from the Fremantle penal colony in Western Australia in 1875. Fenian leaders too were remembered in song long after their abortive rising of 1867.

With the advent of the Land War (to secure tenants' rights and eventual ownership) in the 1870s, Land League marching bands were formed to parade at campaign rallies and meetings. Newspaper reports of evictions in the 1880s refer to many of these bands and the 'national' airs they played to muster support for land agitation. Marching bands had enjoyed a long tradition in political and social movements in Ireland. Orange fife-and-drum bands in the north of Ireland traced their origins back to the Battle of the Boyne in 1690. In the 1830s, marching bands participated in Daniel O'Connell's monster meetings, while Fr Mathew's Temperance Movement helped to create bands in most county towns from 1838 onwards. By the end of the century, many rural parishes had fife-and-drum bands that played at hurling matches, election meetings and religious celebrations. Some, like the Kilfenora Fife and Drum Band in north Clare, were trained by British army bandmasters from nearby garrison towns. These civilian bands were responsible in their own way for the spread of musical literacy among some traditional players. Oral history recalls musicians marching with local fife-and-drum bands by day, and playing for country house dances by night.

Songsmiths and balladeers also captured the front-line tribulations of the Land War and its affiliated Home Rule movement. Land grabbing, boycotting, and tenants' rights found a voice in songs like 'The Wife of the Bold Tenant Farmer', 'The Behy Eviction' and 'Grabbers and Graziers', while Ireland's 'uncrowned king', Charles Stewart Parnell, was eulogised in the ballad 'The Blackbird of Sweet Avondale'. The hornpipe 'The Home Ruler' probably dates from the same era.

New musical instruments arrived in Ireland during the closing decades of the last century. English and German-made concertinas became common household items, especially in western areas. This small hexagonal invention was first adopted as a parlour curiosity in Victorian England and went on to became a maritime instrument. It found its way to places like Clare, Limerick and Kerry in the 1880s, imported by river traffic heading up the Shannon to Limerick, one of the last ports of call for tall ships heading westwards across the Atlantic. The concertina replaced the pipes as a household instrument, especially among female players.

POST-FAMINE COLLECTORS

Despite the watershed of the Great Famine, there was a dynamic interest in collecting and publishing traditional music during the middle decades of the last century. The Society for the Preservation and Publication of the Melodies of Ireland was the first organisation to focus on this task. It was founded by the antiquarian George Petrie in 1851. Petrie had travelled the country during the 1830s, indexing placenames and surveying historical monuments with Eugene O'Curry for the Ordnance Survey Commission. This project gave him a unique opportunity to meet traditional musicians in rural areas. With the help of O'Curry, who was a native Irish speaker, Petrie transcribed hundreds of songs and dance tunes. His small society hoped to create a music archive in Dublin which would act as a deposit box for local collectors throughout the country. Its archive ambitions were never realised, but it eventually published Petrie's *Ancient Music of Ireland* in 1855. Much of Petrie's work was published in 1902-5 by Sir Charles Stanford in a collection containing 195 airs which Petrie received from Patrick Weston Joyce of Glensheen, Co Limerick. Joyce began collecting in Munster in the 1850s at the suggestion of Petrie and published his *Ancient Irish Music* in 1873. He also published *Irish Music and Song* in 1886, and another collection entitled *Old Irish Folk Music and Songs* in 1909.

Other collectors were active in the field, although much of their work never made it into print. Among the more insightful of these was Cork musician William Forde, who collected in Munster and north Connacht during the 1840s. Travelling among informants during the height of the famine, Forde adapted a very systematic approach to his collection, which he hoped to publish with a dissertation on the history of the music. Regrettably, he failed to secure patrons for his project and it never reached print. After his untimely death in London in 1850 his work passed into the hands of John Edward Pigot, son of the Lord Chief Baron of the Exchequer. Pigot was also a collector with over 3,000 unpublished pieces of music in his collection. Another collector of note was Dr Henry Hudson who was born in Dublin in 1798. His collection contained 870 tunes, 137 of which were transcribed from the blind Galway piper Patrick Connelly. One of the most qualified of the contemporary collectors was the clergyman James Goodman who was born near Ventry on the Dingle peninsula in 1839. A musically literate piper, Goodman also spoke fluent Irish. After graduating from Trinity College, Dublin, he was appointed to a Protestant curacy near Skibbereen, Co Cork. Goodman, who became Professor of Irish at Trinity College in 1884, compiled four volumes of traditional music in the period 1860-66.

CULTURAL RENAISSANCE IN THE 1890S

The second Celtic revival reached its apex in the closing decades of the nineteenth century with the establishment of the Gaelic League *(Conradh na Gaeilge)*, the Gaelic Athletic Association (GAA) and the literary revival movement. As well as focusing on the Irish language, the Gaelic League also turned its attention towards a romantic reconstruction of Irish music, song and dance. Established by Douglas Hyde and Eoin McNeill in 1893, the movement quickly spread throughout urban Ireland, as well as to Irish immigrant communities in England and the United States. Its first *céilí* was held in London in 1897. (The term *céilí* was commonly used in Highland Scotland. The terms *cuaird* and *swaree* – from the French *soirée* – were more common in rural Ireland.) The Gaelic League also laid down rules for dancing, and initiated the unprecedented practice of music and singing competitions. In contrast to the spontaneous set dancing of rural Ireland, the figure dances of the Gaelic League céilí were formal and formulaic. Strict decorum and good taste were observed. In 1897 the *Feis Ceoil* was established by Dr AW Patterson, and the Gaelic League held its first Oireachtas. The latter was confined to competitions in Irish music, whereas the former was influenced by English competitive festivals and was open to classical and traditional performers.

While urban Ireland was enjoying its cultural renaissance, a chasm of indifference often separated it from more traditional lifestyles west of the Shannon, where some unique dialects of dance music still prevailed. By the early 1900s, some cultural nationalists believed that set dancing was 'foreign' and 'improper'. Conversely, country-house musicians had little contact with the literate urban atmosphere of the *feis ceoil*. Their music followed the work cycle of the *meitheal* – a cooperative group of farm workers – and the ritual gatherings of the agricultural year. Inherent within their lifestyle was an ongoing cycle of 'American Wakes', during which departing emigrants were fêted by friends and neighbours. This haemorrhage of emigration continued to displace Irish traditional music well into the new century. With extended families in America, traditional musicians in the West of Ireland often found it easier to identify with the Irish music scene in Boston and Chicago than with the cultural renaissance in urban Ireland.

PROFILE: THE BLIND PIPER GARRETT BARRY

Garrett Barry was born into an Irish-speaking community in Inagh, Co Clare in 'Black '47', the worst year of the Great Famine. Exposed to famine sickness and malnutrition as a child, he contracted small pox and remained blind for the rest of his life. In keeping with the tradition of giving the handicapped a legitimate role in their community, particularly in the folk arts, Garrett was given an opportunity to learn the uilleann pipes. This guaranteed him status and a livelihood among the mountainy farmers of west Clare until his death in 1899.

Patronised in a community where tradition-bearers were highly respected, Garrett travelled throughout west Clare playing for house dances and other festive occasions. His performance at a house dance usually involved a solo repertoire of slow airs, dance tunes and piping 'pieces'. According to local folklore, other musicians were expected to play for sets in the kitchen, leaving Garrett to sample the finest hospitality of the house, 'up in the room' or parlour with the senior members of the family. Among the tunes associated with him are 'Garrett Barry's Jig', 'The Humours of Glen', 'Garrett Barry's Mazurka' and 'I Buried My Wife and Danced on Top of Her'. All of these dance tunes are still part of the vernacular folk tradition in Clare.

QUEBEC TO THE KLONDIKE: THE FAMINE DIASPORA

Ireland's population declined from 8.5 million to just under 6 million in the ten-year period from 1845 to 1855. This catastrophic decline resulted from hunger, disease and involuntary emigration. Ireland's crisis however was not a socio-economic anomaly. It was more a dire symptom of the country's forced integration into a market economy, supplying raw materials, goods and cheap labour to Great Britain, the world's leading industrial nation of the day.

In the decade that followed the Great Famine, almost thirty percent of the population emigrated. With the exception of famine 'criminals' transported to Van Dieman's Land, and orphans dispatched to Australia, the majority of Ireland's famine emigrants chose to cross the North Atlantic, many in the notorious coffin ships. The trans-Atlantic crossing to Quebec was the cheapest, until the Canadian authorities levied a poll tax on emigrants to defray the cost of caring for them. A passage at the height of the famine cost twelve to fifteen dollars for a six- to eight-week crossing below decks in an overcrowded vessel. On arrival, many passengers found conditions little better than those which they had left behind in Ireland. Widespread disease and destitution had become intractable problems. Quarantine stations were quickly established to deal with the crisis, the most horrendous being Grosse Île on the St Lawrence, where thousands of famine victims were buried in mass graves, within sight of their new homeland.

IRISH TRADITIONAL MUSIC IN QUEBEC

Deprived of their audiences in Ireland, throngs of traditional musicians followed their bedraggled patrons into exile, some to struggle as anonymous street players, others to thrive as celebrated figures in an emergent music hall industry. The expanding cities of the United States claimed most of these musicians. Others however settled in Quebec and contributed to its diverse storehouse of music and dance. The Irish had become established in Quebec well before the influx of famine victims. Irish 'Wild Geese' soldiers in the armies of France were given land grants in Quebec during the eighteenth century. By 1851 the city boasted an Irish population of 9,120 – an 800 percent increase in thirty years. Most of the new arrivals were famine emigrants, among them thousands of orphans adopted by Quebecois families.

Irish traditional music and dance became important elements in the process of integrating with francophone culture in Quebec. Group dances such as the *'Quadrille Frangais'*, the *'Saratoga'*, the *'Lancier'*, and the *'Calédonia'* became extremely popular in rural Quebec during the middle decades of the nineteenth century. Consisting of five or six different figures, these quadrille sets bore an uncanny resemblance to their 'Lancer' and 'Caledonian' counterparts in rural Ireland. Solo dances like the Quebecois *'gigue'* emerged from a fusion of Irish *sean nós* steps and English clogging at the beginning of the last century. Still respected today in areas like Saguenay, Charlevoix, the Beauce and Estrie, the *'gigue'* dancer is expected to keep the upper body rigid, straight and balanced. The same traditional posture is also expected from his counterpart in the West of Ireland.

Dance tunes also bear evidence of the Irish presence in Quebec. The celebrated Quebecois fiddler Jean Carignan recorded a variety of Irish dance tunes, many from the Sligo-based repertoire of Michael Coleman. Old-style melodeon player Keith Corrigan still plays archaic settings of tunes which have changed little since they were introduced by Irish immigrants in the nineteenth century. Corrigan's rhythmical single-note style can still be heard in Irish-Quebecois communities like Valcartier, Saint-Patrice-de-Beaurivage and Shannon. His repertoire includes old settings of 'St Anne's Reel' and *'Le Rêve du Diable'*, which is known in Ireland as 'The Devil among the Tailors'.

IRISH MUSIC IN URBAN AMERICA

East-coast cities from Boston to Baltimore claimed the largest influx of famine emigrants. What work they could find was usually menial, rigorous and poorly paid. Most of them exchanged their rural backgrounds for unfamiliar urban settings and often suffered ethnic discrimination from the white Anglo-Saxon Protestant establishment. The prejudice of the 'No Irish Need Apply' signs did not go unanswered by the immigrant scribes of the day:

> I'm a decent lad just landed from the town of
> Ballinafad;
> I want a situation and I want it very bad.
> I've seen employment advertised. 'It's just the thing,'
> says I,
> But the dirty spalpeen ended with
> 'No Irish need apply.'
> 'Whoo,' says I, 'that is an insult, but to get the place
> I'll try.'
> So I went there to see the blackguard with his
> 'No Irish Need Apply.'

Despite their trials and tribulations, alienation and loneliness, the emigrant Irish continued to pour into the sprawling ghettos of industrial America. By 1850 twenty-six percent of the population of New York and twenty-five percent of the population of Chicago were Irish born. By 1855, there were one-and-a-half million Irish-born people living in the United States.

Although fifty-four percent of famine emigrants were from Irish-speaking districts, most of the songs which survived in their new communities were sung in English. These offer a tapestry of insights into Irish American life, from the abysmal experience of the ghetto, to the comfort of domestic service, and the proliferation of Irish fraternities in urban America. The role of Irish workers in the formation of American labour unions is clearly documented in song, not least the clandestine activities of the Molly Maguires, who represented the anthracite miners of Pennsylvania in the 1860s. Ballads like 'Paddy Works on the Railroad', 'Drill, Ye Tarriers, Drill' and 'We're Bound for San Diego' index the migration of Irish workers along the canals and railroads of the industrial frontier. Other songs highlight the contribution of Irish immigrants to American wars during the middle decades of the last century. 'Green Grows the Laurel' recalls the Irish contribution to the Mexican-American War of 1845-47. (It has been suggested that the Mexican term *gringo* derives from the title of this song, such was its popularity along the front line.) Later on, 'Paddy's Lamentation' rued the drafting of immigrants into the Union army during the Civil War, which claimed the lives of 150,000 Irishmen.

In the years following the American Civil War, the western frontier began to attract new settlers, industry started to boom, and urban life teemed with new entertainment. Irish music became a veritable asset in the music hall industry, where audiences were comprised mainly of immigrants. Between 1840 and 1880, minstrel companies employed thousands of Irish performers, who helped to create steps like the 'Soft Shoe Shuffle' and the 'Buck and Wing' from a combination of Irish and African-American dances. However, the new political ethos in post-Civil War America took a dim view of blackface comedy. This genre, with its comic depiction of southern plantation life, was soon supplanted by variety theatre and, eventually, by vaudeville.

Variety theatre was an eclectic mix of novelty acts, acrobatics, music and comedy. It provided employment for thousands of Irish musicians, singers and stand-up comics, albeit in the profane ambience of the concert saloon, where alcohol played a major part in the proceedings. Variety also gave full vent to the buffoonery of the stage Irishman, which had been a stock motif in English drama since the seventeenth century. By the 1870s, however, the raucous impropriety of the concert saloon gave way to vaudeville, a more refined form of variety entertainment which took place in alcohol-free establishments. This new genre was to have a profound effect on American popular culture and dominated the course of Irish music in urban America for the next half-century.

THE VAUDEVILLE EXPERIENCE

If minstrel and variety shows thrived on Irish music, vaudeville also prospered from the same source. Irish songs and dance tunes were plunged again into the melting pot during the vaudevillian era, and re-emerged in a variety of commercial forms. The most celebrated icon of the period was George M Cohen, known as 'Mr Yankee Doodle Dandy', the son of Irish famine immigrants, whose hits 'Give my Regards to Broadway' and 'You're a Grand Old Flag' became anthems for generations of Americans from their first performance in 1904. Song-writer Johnny Patterson also became a household name among Irish immigrants during the same period. Patterson had left Clare to join the British army after the famine. He eventually became a circus performer in the US and enjoyed considerable notoriety during the 1870s and 1880s. Filled with images of exile and a sentimental longing for home, his songs include 'Good Bye, Johnny Dear', 'Bridget Donahue', 'The Hat My Father Wore', 'Shake Hands With Your Uncle Dan' and 'The Stone Outside Dan Murphy's Door', the latter inspired by his orphan childhood in Old Mill Street, Ennis, in the 1850s.

By the turn of the century, citadels of industry like New York, Boston and Chicago were thriving centres of Irish traditional music. A string of pipers' clubs crossed the country from Philadelphia to San Francisco. Vaudeville employed hundreds of Irish musicians, and novel changes like the development of concert-pitch pipes, perfected by the Taylor Brothers, made uilleann pipes more suitable for large concert hall audiences. As the Irish moved up the social ladder in urban America, so too did their music-makers. The lace-curtain Irish were also cultivating a taste for 'high art'. Rising opera stars such as tenor John

McCormack were invited to perform in America. McCormack made his first US appearance at the World's Fair in St Louis in 1904. He did not stay very long however. Incensed by the stage-Irish routines of vaudevillians like piper Patsy Touhey, he left St Louis in a well-publicised huff, and did not return to America again until 1909. McCormack's 'flight back to propriety' did little to diminish his popularity among Irish-Americans. By the 1920s, his Victor Red Seal recordings enjoyed a sanctimonious presence in most Irish-American homes.

Recording technology also caught the attention of Irish traditional musicians on the vaudeville circuit. By the 1890s, Thomas Edison's recording machine had been improved further by the Victor and Columbia recording companies and cylindrical recordings were issued commercially. New York piper Billy Hannafin was one of the first Irish musicians to record on cylinder, in 1898. He played two reels, 'The Salamanca' and 'The Colliers'. The virtuoso piper Patsy Touhey also recorded his classic renditions of 'Miss McLeod's Reel' and 'The Flogging Reel' on cylinder in the early 1900s. It was not long before other musicians followed their lead.

IRISH MUSICIANS IN THE AMERICAN WEST

Although most famine immigrants settled in urban America, others built rural communities in the Ottawa River Valley in Ontario and along the Miramichi Valley in New Brunswick. More travelled west across the Great Plains to the Rocky Mountains and to Texas, before it became part of the United States. The Irish settlements of San Patricio and Refugio were both founded in the 1830s, when the region was still part of Mexico. With each new wave of settlement, Irish traditional music contributed to the social life of the host community – in Canadian lumber camps, Texan farmsteads, and frontier towns in the American West.

The first Irish who moved west were guides and

trappers such as Luther 'Yellowstone' Kelly, who explored the vast mountain wilderness between Dakota and the Rockies. The lure of gold soon opened the floodgates. Thousands of Irish poured over the Sierras in 1849 when gold was discovered in California.

By the turn of the century, Irish traditional music and dance enjoyed considerable patronage in San Francisco. Members of the Gaelic Dancing Club performed frequently at Gaelic League events, and the self-styled Professor Batt Scanlon was the 'leading exponent of Irish music in the west'. San Francisco had its own pipers' club by the end of the 1890s, and a sufficiently impressive store of music to warrant a collection of tunes by Dr MC O'Toole, a well-known Irish physician in the city. Unfortunately, the 1906 earthquake put an abrupt end to the pipers' club and to O'Toole's collection of Irish music.

Long before the charitable Choctaw tribe sent money to the victims of the Great Famine, Irish traditional musicians had been sharing their music with Native Americans. By the early 1800s French-Canadians, Scots and Irishmen who worked for the Hudson Bay Company had introduced fiddle music to the native peoples of Canada. Dance tunes like 'Haste to the Wedding', 'Soldier's Joy', 'Drops of Brandy', 'The Devil's Dream', 'The Irish Washerwoman' and 'The Fisher's Hornpipe' were played by Native Americans from the Mi'qMak in Nova Scotia, to the Saulteaux, Algonkians and inter-racial Métis in Manitoba. By the end of the century, Orcadian fiddling, a composite of Norse, Scottish and Irish fiddling played in the Orkney Islands, enjoyed widespread popularity among the Athabaskan people in Alaska's Interior – a lasting legacy of Orcadians who worked for the Hudson Bay Company. This emergent tradition was further augmented by Irish miners during the Klondike Gold Rush in the 1890s. Irish fiddlers who made their way to the Yukon in search of gold played for fellow prospectors in

Dawson City, Fort Yukon and Fairbanks. They also shared tunes, dances and playing styles with native Alaskans.

A century later, some striking similarities still exist between Irish and Athabaskan dance music. Both genres are played for set dancing – quadrilles and contra dancing are popular in Athabaskan communities – and both are still passed on through a process of oral transmission. As well as favouring slides and double-stops to ornament their music, the Athabaskans use lilting techniques to memorise tunes before transferring them to instruments. Like many older set dancers in Ireland, Athabaskan dancers favour 'close to the floor' stepping styles. Fiddler Arthur Kennedy, who lived in the Koyukon village of Galena, regarded himself as an 'Irish-Athabaskan'. His repertoire included Irish dance tunes as well as American old-time music. Celebrated Athabaskan fiddler Bill Stevens, who has been a guest performer with the Chieftains, readily acknowledges the localised Irish tunes in his repertoire.

IRISH MUSIC IN LOWLAND SCOTLAND

The nineteenth century saw a steady stream of human traffic between west Ulster and the industrial cities of the Clyde Valley. The industrial revolution in Scotland attracted factory workers from Donegal and Derry, as well as from Fermanagh, Sligo, Leitrim and Mayo. Fishery workers from areas as far west as the Rosses in Donegal travelled to Lerwick on the Shetland Islands, where they found seasonal work salting herrings. Migrant farm workers also made the annual crossing to work as 'tattie hookers' (potato diggers) in the tillage farms of Lowland Scotland. This recurring exodus included a number of musicians. Mixing with migrant musicians from the Highlands, the tattie hookers formed 'bothy bands'. These groups took their name from the Gaelic *bothán* or hut, referring to the huts where the potato workers lived while on seasonal hire.

The autobiography of *sean nós* singer Róise Rua Nic Gríanna from Arranmore Island, Co Donegal, recalls the music of the bothy bands. Known on Arranmore as '*Róise na nAmhrán*' (Róise of the Songs), the singer travelled with the potato squads to Scotland as a young woman. She remembered that 'there were very few squads that didn't have a fiddler with them at that time. We would often have dances in the bothies, and people from the other squads could come and visit us, or we would go to them when they had something similar. The old dances were the most common ones we would look for; the sets, the "Lancers", the "Maggie Piggy", the "[Shoe the] Donkey", the "Mazurka", the "Barn Dance" and their likes. Often as well, we would be interested in learning the Scottish dances: the "Gay Gordons", the "Highland", the "Corn Rigs" and others.' From these bothy sessions, dance tunes and fiddle styles from the Highlands were absorbed and adapted by the indigenous traditions of Ulster. This bothy tradition accounts for the prevalence of 'highlands' (dance tunes in 4/4 time adapted from 'strathspeys') in Donegal. It may also explain the single-stroke staccato bowing style which distinguishes the fiddling of the region today.

IRISH MUSIC IN ENGLAND

The decade between 1845 and 1855 saw 200-300,000 Irish settle permanently in Britain. During the height of the Great Famine, droves of destitute Irish crowded into port cities like Glasgow, Liverpool and London, where they packed into working-class slums and shanties. The impoverished famine Irish did not assimilate easily into their new environs. Many of the social problems which confronted their contemporaries in America were also evident in England. Lack of industrial training and language skills combined with poverty and poor health to keep the Irish on the economic fringe of British society. They sought jobs on building sites, railways, mines and dockyards; their families crammed into dilapidated tenements and red-brick terraces from the mining towns of Lancashire to the dockyard ghettoes of Greater London.

Being Irish and Catholic in a racially hostile environment, famine immigrants had little loyalty to their British hosts. After years of tenacity and entrenchment, they succeeded in creating self-sustaining communities, many beyond the mainframe of British culture. They also formed a network of social clubs and societies. Many of these grew out of religious fraternities in Irish Catholic parishes. Others were an expression of nationalist fervour and were explicitly political in character. By the end of the century cultural nationalism was making a significant impact through the newly-established Gaelic League, which found willing converts among the Irish in Britain.

Music and dancing played a major role in League gatherings. The first céilí held by the League was organised by its London branch on 30 October 1897. It took place in the Bloomsbury Hall near the British Museum, and the programme included music, songs and stepdancing. Music was provided by Fitzgerald's Band who played jigs, waltzes and quadrille sets. The arrangement of dancers facing each other in two lines for group dances like the 'Haymaker's Jig' was conceived at this céilí. This line-out was probably influenced by Scottish céilí dancing, which was popular among Scottish migrants in industrial England.

By the turn of the century London had become a haven of Irish writers, singers, musicians and dancing masters. Rosmuc writer Pádraic Ó Conaire, who vividly portrayed the emotional hardship of the Irish immigrant in London, worked in the British civil service before returning to Ireland in 1914. His short story '*Go hUair a Bháis*', ('Until the Hour of his Death'), first appeared in 1904 in *Guth na nGaedheal* ('The Voice of the Gael'), an Irish-language magazine published by the London branch of the Gaelic

League. Francis Fahy, a native of Kinvara, Co Galway, also worked as a civil servant in London. He was a founding member of The Irish Literary Society and was also president of the first Gaelic League branch in London. He is remembered for his ballad 'The Ould Plaid Shawl' and for various English translations of Irish songs. The Irish Folk Song Society was founded in London in 1903. Among its luminaries was the writer and folksong collector Alfred Perceval Graves, father of the poet and novelist Robert Graves. Kerry dancing master Patrick Reidy lived in Hackney. He contributed 'The High Caul Cap', *'An Rince Fada'* and the four- and eight-hand reels to *A Handbook of Irish Dances*, published in 1902. Reidy taught Irish dancing at the Bijou Theatre near the Strand.

The London Irish were at their most controversial when they began to 'legitimise' Irish dances. In an attempt to avoid confusion with Scottish *céilithe*, enthusiasts like Fionán Mac Coluim and 'Professor' Patrick Reidy set out to create a canon of 'authentic' Irish dances. This would separate Irish from Scottish dances, and also weed out 'foreign elements' in the Irish dance tradition. Determined to ignore the archaic common ground between Scottish and Irish dances, a group from the London branch of the Gaelic League came to Ireland to collect various dances from 'authentic' sources. Much of their field trip was confined to Kerry, because of its traditional association with dancing masters since the late eighteenth century. In their resulting evaluation, the group came to regard Munster dances and stepping styles as being 'superior', while northern and western dances were discouraged. The *sean nós* dancing style of Connemara, which was more flat-footed than its Munster counterpart, and involved grandiose arm movements, was seriously frowned upon. Quadrille sets, waltzes, barn dances and *schottisches*, which were all regarded as 'foreign imports', also met with disapproval. Henceforth, the Munster style of dancing became a prime barometer for an emerging canon of national dances – a canon which has endured for most of a century.

The preoccupation with céilí dancing also made way for other parallel developments. The Céilí band in its present form was a product of the London-Irish dance scene. The term was probably coined by Frank Lee's Tara Céilí Band which was set up to play for a dance in Notting Hill's Sarsfield Club on Saint Patrick's Day, 1918. The venue, complete with resident dancing master Pádraig O'Keane, had been established as an Irish club in 1890.

Of the music-makers who left Ireland with the famine diaspora, only a minority rose to prominence in their host countries. Thousands more passed quietly into oblivion. In the period 1856-1921, Ireland lost between 4.1 and 4.5 million inhabitants, including one million unrecorded emigrants to Great Britain. Three million emigrated to the United States and Canada, while an additional 289,000 sailed to Australia and New Zealand. Sixty thousand more went to South Africa, Brazil, Argentina and elsewhere. Much of the music of the Irish diaspora to other parts of the world still awaits serious investigation.

PROFILE: FRANCIS O'NEILL

Flute player Francis O'Neill was born in Tralibane, outside Bantry in west Cork, in 1848. He grew up in a rural community that had just emerged from the horrors of the Great Famine. His childhood was spent in the social distress of post-famine Ireland, with its ongoing procession of American wakes, heartless evictions and abrupt cultural changes. O'Neill's family expected him to study for the priesthood. However, at the age of sixteen he ran away from home, reached Cork city and signed on as a cabin boy on board a merchant ship bound for Boston.

After four years at sea, including a shipwreck in the Pacific, O'Neill arrived in San Francisco. He worked as a shepherd, a schoolteacher in Missouri, a sailor on the

Great Lakes and a policeman in Chicago, finally becoming Chief Superintendent of Police in 1901. His senior rank however was short lived. Political expediency within the Democratic Party cut short his career, and he resigned in 1905.

Francis O'Neill had an abiding love of traditional music. This had been cultivated during his childhood in west Cork, and whetted in Chicago towards the end of the last century. In the early 1880s he met James O'Neill, a fiddler from Co Down, who had a huge store of dance tunes and an uncommon ability to write music. The two O'Neills formed a lifelong friendship, both as police colleagues and avid collectors of traditional dance music. Their immediate sources were musicians within the Irish community in Chicago, many of whom were members of the city's police force. After two decades of collecting, O'Neill published *The Music of Ireland* in 1903. Despite its transcription faults, O'Neill's work contained the largest collection of dance tunes ever published. His 1,850 pieces included 1,100 dance tunes (as against Petrie's 300, and Bunting's meagre handful). In 1907, O'Neill published a second collection, *The Dance Music of Ireland,* which contained 1,001 tunes. This volume won immediate acceptance, and still enjoys a biblical status among traditional musicians. Other collections followed, among them *Irish Music* and *Waifs and Strays of Gaelic Melody.* The former included piano accompaniments, a feature which confirmed the new drawing room tastes of the lace-curtain Irish in Chicago.

In 1906 Francis O'Neill and his Clare-born wife Anna Rogers spent six weeks in Ireland. While there, he collected a number of dance tunes from players like Johnny Allen and Paddy MacNamara in east Clare. However, he was not impressed by the lack of respect shown to traditional musicians, especially in urban Ireland. On returning to Chicago he began work on *Irish*

Folk Music: A Fascinating Hobby, which he published in 1910. It contains an unprecedented store of information about Irish music history, based on written and oral sources. The ethnobiographical process which he began in *Irish Folk Music* continued in *Irish Minstrels and Musicians,* a lavish collection of essays on pipers, harpers and collectors, published in 1913. Correspondents from all over North America, Ireland and Australia contributed to this volume, which contained a large collection of contemporary photographs, transcriptions and songs.

Despite charges that O'Neill may have drawn too freely, and without acknowledgement, on *Ryan's Mammoth Collection,* collected and edited by William Bradbury Ryan of Boston in 1883, his contributions vastly outrank the combined work of his predecessors. His goal was to 'immortalise the forgotten though deserving musicians of Ireland'. To this end, he succeeded. In recording the cultural circumstances of his sources, O'Neill provided a unique spotlight on Irish-American society undergoing a phenomenal period of transition in the New World.

RECORDS, RADIOS AND HALLS: 'THE NEW CENTURY'

A strange blend of rural decay and urban renewal marked the status of Irish traditional music in the early years of the twentieth century. The role of the musician in isolated areas west of the Shannon was very different from that of his contemporary in urban Ireland. Similarly, his sparse subsistence lifestyle had little in common with the progressive mores of bourgeois Dublin or Cork.

THE MUSIC OF TOWN AND COUNTRY

In the interim between the Boer War of 1898 and the

outbreak of World War I, Ireland experienced an exceptional period of economic stability. By the end of the 1890s the Gaelic League had built up a network of branches throughout the country. Its primary role was to revive the Irish language, which had been undermined by the National School system and the Great Famine. Language classes were set up by the League's *timirí* (travelling teachers) who taught all over the country. Some *timirí,* like Cork piper Donncha Ó Laoghaire, who taught Irish in west Clare, were accomplished musicians and took a discerning interest in the music of the regions where they worked. Irish figure or céilí dancing (as opposed to 'foreign imported' set dancing) was also the preserve of the Gaelic League. This was promoted initially for *feis* competitions, but eventually became the main style of dance for all social events organised by the League. The League's quest for an 'authentic' Irish dance costume also began around this time. Within a short period, this costume changed from simple cloaks and sashes to silver buckle shoes, brooches and other nationalist emblems.

Running parallel with the language movement was the GAA, which had set up a myriad of hurling and football clubs, especially in rural parishes, by the turn of the century. Separatist in outlook, the GAA insisted that its members should avoid foreign games. This credo was also endemic in the Irish Ireland philosophy propagated by DP Moran in *The Leader*. In 1905 he wrote that 'the foundation of Ireland is the Gael, and the Gael must be the element that absorbs'. Less polemic, but equally passionate in its own nationalist rhetoric, was the literary renaissance powered by Yeats and Lady Gregory in the 1890s.

The centenary of the 1798 rebellion was marked by parades and cultural events in many parts of the country. In March 1898, the first pipers' club in Ireland was founded in Cork by Seán Wayland. It catered for uilleann pipers as well as war-pipers (who played mouth-blown bagpipes, as opposed to elbow-blown uilleann pipes). Its marching band was the first in Ireland to wear kilts. Other cities soon followed Cork's example and founded their own pipers' clubs. In June 1898 PJ McCall eulogised the Wexford rebellion in his famous ballad 'Boolavogue' which appeared in the *Irish Weekly Independent*. Seven years afterwards in 1905, Grattan Flood's seminal *History of Irish Music* helped to bring Irish music and song closer to the mainframe of the cultural renaissance in urban Ireland.

Politics too was experiencing a vibrant period of innovation. In 1898 the Local Government Act revitalised political activity at local level, while shortly afterwards Arthur Griffith's *United Irishman* voiced the novel credos of economic nationalism and dual monarchy. From 1905 onwards, his new Sinn Féin ('ourselves alone') party attracted members from the Irish Republican Brotherhood (IRB) and other separatist groups preparing for insurrection.

IRISH-AMERICAN GRAMOPHONE RECORDINGS

With the exception of wax cylindrical recordings made by pipers Patsy Touhey and Billy Hannafin, the earliest recordings of Irish traditional music to enjoy widespread circulation in the United States came from Charles D'Almaine, Joseph Samuels, John Witzmann and Leopold Moeslein, all of whom were non-Irish studio violinists. They played bland, unornamented versions of Irish dance tunes, taken directly from published transcriptions. The only non-Irish performer to show any discerning familiarity with an Irish traditional style was the German-American accordionist John Kimmel, whose celebrated recording career lasted from 1904 to 1920. The recording of Irish dance music by Irish performers in America began in earnest in 1916, a pivotal year in Irish political history. The force behind this enterprise was Ellen O'Byrne de Witt, a

New York music seller and travel agent, who arranged to have Eddie Herborn and James Wheeler, an accordion and banjo duet, recorded by Columbia Records. The success of this seminal 78rpm recording, which featured 'The Stack of Barley', was enough to convince the American record industry that a huge untapped Irish-American market lay right on their doorstep.

In 1919 Patrick Clancy cut four medleys for the Victor Talking Machine Company and became the first Irish fiddler to record for a consumer audience. By the late 1920s the nascent US recording industry had attracted celebrities like fiddlers Michael Coleman, James Morrison and Paddy Killoran from Sligo, accordionist Petie Conlon from Galway, concertina player William J Mullaly from Westmeath and the famous Flanagan Brothers from Waterford City. All of these were to have a profound longterm influence on Irish traditional music on both sides of the North Atlantic.

MUSIC AND THE BIRTH OF THE FREE STATE

Sinn Féin's armed rebellion of 1916 sparked off a chain of political transformations in Ireland. In 1917 Sinn Féin defeated the Irish Parliamentary Party in a series of by-elections and almost completely replaced them in the general election of 1918. In January 1919 the Sinn Féin deputies, who had refused to take their seats in Westminster, reconstituted themselves in Dublin as *Dáil Eireann* (the Assembly of Ireland). The British attempt to crush Sinn Féin led to the War of Independence during which the IRA, led by Michael Collins, waged a successful guerrilla campaign against the police and the notorious Black and Tans – ex-soldiers wearing a mix of police and army uniforms. The British Prime Minister, Lloyd George, eventually sought a compromise in the Government of Ireland Act, which became law in December 1920. The following year, the Anglo-Irish treaty was signed. Under its terms, twenty-six counties gained independence as the

'Irish Free State', but still remained within the British Commonwealth. Six of Ulster's counties had already been granted their own assembly by the Government of Ireland Act and remained part of the United Kingdom. The establishment of the Free State was followed immediately by a bitter civil war between government forces and those sections of the IRA which opposed the treaty. Although a truce was negotiated in May 1923, the civil war left a legacy of hatred which was to affect the emergent state for several generations.

The revolutionary state envisioned by Pádraig Pearse was nowhere to be seen during the first decade of Free State Ireland. The War of Independence and the Civil War left much of the country with chronic social and economic problems. Despite its structural defects however, the new state quickly won the support of merchants and shopkeepers, well-off farmers, clerics and middle-class professionals, all of whom had a vested interest in the benefits of stability. It was not long before this bourgeois core, which had a long pedigree in Irish history, sired a repressive Ireland governed by an overwhelming social and cultural conservatism. In 1923 the Censorship of Films Act was passed. It was followed six years later by the Censorship of Publications Act. This edict, which purged two generations of writers from the country, had been orchestrated by the Irish Vigilance Societies and the Catholic Truth Society of Ireland. The same Catholic inquisition soon turned its attention towards Irish traditional music.

In rural Ireland, where the Black and Tans had broken up house dances three years previously, congregations, including musicians and dancers, were reminded by their priests during Lent 1924 that 'The Irish bishops in their Lenten pastorals refer to the existence of many abuses. Chief among these may be mentioned women's fashions, immodest dress, indecent dancing, theatrical performances and cinema exhibitions, evil literature, drink, strikes and lockouts.' Unsupervised dancing, motor cars, jazz and unlicensed dance halls all qualified for particular condemnation. In his pastoral letter of 1931, Cardinal Mac Rory pointed out the dangers of too much mobility. 'Even the present travelling facilities make a difference. By bicycle, motor car and bus, boys and girls can now travel great distances to dances, with the result that a dance in the quietest country parish may be attended by unsuitables from a distance.' It would only be a matter of time before 'unsupervised' house dances faced the legal wrath of church and state.

In 1926, the Free State ventured into the precarious domain of radio in its efforts to consolidate national identity. Radio was initially an urban phenomenon in Ireland. It made inroads into rural communities and become very popular when it began broadcasting hurling and football matches. Oral history in rural parishes still recalls crowds of hushed supporters gathered around a 'wireless' left on a windowsill to hear Mícheál Ó hEithir's breath-taking commentaries in the 1930s and 1940s. The first director of 2RN, as the new station was called until Radio Eireann appeared in 1937, was Séamus Clandillon, an Irish language and music enthusiast who soon began to invite traditional musicians to play live on the radio. Radio news magazines occasionally carried photographs and details about these musicians. In July 1927, the term 'céilí trio' was used in the *Irish Radio Review* to describe Dick Smith's trio of fiddle, flute and piano which broadcast a series of weekly 'recitals' on 2RN. The earliest evidence of a céilí band playing on 2RN came to light in March 1929 when the *Irish Radio News* announced a broadcast by Leo Molloy's Céilí Band. One of the first solo performers to play to the nation on 2RN was accordion player Michael Grogan from Winetown, Co Westmeath. He made five live broadcasts from Dublin in 1928.

THE BALLINAKILL TRADITIONAL PLAYERS

By far the most dynamic ensemble to play on 2RN in its early years was the Ballinakill Traditional Players from east Galway. By 1926 the campaign to rid the countryside of jazz was 'in full swing'. Finding a novel solution to safeguard the morality of his parishioners, Fr Tom Larkin created the Ballinakill Traditional Players (later known as the Ballinakill Céilí Band) to play for céilí dances in the Ballinakill and Woodford areas of east Galway.

The band, which was drawn from a small farming community where house dancing was popular, consisted mainly of flute players and fiddlers. Flute players Stephen Maloney and Tommy Whelan as well as fiddlers Tommy White, Kevin Maloney, Aggie White and Jerry Maloney all played by ear. The literate exception was piano player Anna Rafferty from Carraroe House, one of Ballinakill's more imposing buildings. Fr Larkin, who was also a fiddler, coached the players, got them to practice common versions of tunes and selected settings which suited their combination of instruments. He also transcribed their repertoire so that the piano player could read the melody line and arrange her own bass chords. Practice and creativity paid off. As well as blending orality and literacy, Fr Larkin's experiment brought together musicians from both ends of the social spectrum in rural Ireland. In 1928 the band played at the Athlone *feis*, where Séamus Clandillon was most impressed by their style and approach to traditional dance tunes. They subsequently made numerous live broadcasts to the nation from 2RN in Dublin. Their first 78rpm recordings were made by Parlophone in 1930. The same company invited them to travel to London in November 1931 to record the now-classic 'Knocknagow' and 'The Fowling Piece' (better known as 'Scotch Mary' and 'The Templehouse' reels). These pioneer recordings became the benchmarks against which other céilí bands (like the nearby Aughrim

Slopes, the Leitrim and the Tulla) rated themselves during the next three decades. The exhilarating music of 'The Old Ballinakill' however, with its delicate blend of flutes and fiddles, and its unique repertoire of tunes and settings, has had few equals since its halcyon days in the 1930s.

IRISH GRAMOPHONE RECORDINGS: 1920s-1930s

If radios were an uncommon luxury in rural Ireland, so too were Victrolas, the wind-up gramophones of the 1920s. Their presence became more common, however, as emigration increased after the War of Independence. Many found their way into country kitchens as part of an emigrant parcel. Others were bought in local towns on fair days. Apart from their novelty value, gramophones met with a mixed response in rural communities. Many musicians welcomed an opportunity to hear new tunes and dialects from players they would never meet within the narrow confines of local sessions and house dances.

Others felt threatened by the sheer mastery of the music on some 78rpm recordings, and consequently abandoned their own playing. Both musical responses eventually led to the decline of regional dialects and nuances. For set dancers on the other hand, the gramophone was both a musical novelty and a practical nuisance. Although the quality of gramophone music was often superior to that of local dance players, it generally stopped playing before the set dance figures ended. Dancers would have to stop dancing, leave the floor and wind up the gramophone again to complete their figure.

Most records bought in Ireland in the 1920s were issued by English companies, initially in domestic catalogues and later in supplements aimed uniquely at the Irish market. These English companies also carried 78rpm records of Irish music made in America. Traditional recordings made in London in the 1920s focused primarily on the revivalist audience affiliated with the Gaelic League. One of the most prolific musicians to be recorded at the time was the piper Leo Rowsome who taught piping at the Dublin College of Music from 1922 until his death in 1970. His legato style of piping with its exuberant use of regulator accompaniment was featured on the Columbia, HMV (His Master's Voice), Decca and Broadcast labels in the 1920s and 1930s. The Waterford piper Liam Walsh was also recorded in London during the same period. The Fingal Trio were recorded in Dublin by Columbia during its third recording trip to Ireland in the summer of 1931. This celebrated ensemble was composed of Dublin piper James Ennis (father of Séamus Ennis), Sligo flute player John Cawley and fiddler Frank O'Higgins, from Kells, Co Meath. O'Higgins (1891-1975) went on to make several solo recordings, especially of set dances, and both his style and repertoire enjoyed much popularity among traditional players in the West of Ireland in the 1940s.

By 1936 companies like EMI Records (Ireland) Ltd had set up recording facilities in Dublin. This move came in the midst of the economic war with England and was designed to explore native talent and promote records made in Ireland. Donegal fiddler Neilie O'Boyle was among the first solo artists to record in an Irish-based studio. Born in Easton, Pennsylvania, O'Boyle moved back to Dungloe, Co Donegal, in 1897. Acknowledged as the composer of 'The Moving Cloud' reel, much of his personalised style was developed while playing music for silent films. In 1937, O'Boyle recorded his unique version of the 'Harvest Home' hornpipe and 'The Green Mountain' reel, as well as a jig selection featuring 'Haste to the Wedding' and 'Over the Hills'. His recordings, along with those of the Kerry fiddler Denis Murphy, are among the few examples of rare regional styles which were recorded during the 78rpm era. These recordings were followed in the 1930s and 1940s by recordings from the Belhaval Trio from Co Leitrim, and the Moate Céilí Band from Co Westmeath. Although both groups represented contrasting regional styles, their dialects were regrettably muted by other commercial recordings and the advent of *fleadh cheoil* competitions in the 1950s.

THE IRISH DANCING COMMISSION

While commercial recordings were slowly changing the geography of Irish dance music, a new regulatory body, An Coimisiún le Rincí Gaelacha (The Irish Dancing Commission), was quickly forging a strict link between nationalism and dancing competitions. Set up by Conradh na Gaeilge (the Gaelic League), the Commission formally codified Irish dancing as a competitive process in 1930. It was formed to exercise control over local as well as national competitions. It also sanctioned all open competitions, authenticated students, certified teachers and authorised adjudicators, so that the same standards were adhered to throughout the Irish dancing world. As well as regulating solo and group dances, the Commission laid down precise rules for national dance costumes, along with the 'proper' type of music and rhythm required for its dancers. Inevitably, set dancers continued to sin in their limbo of 'foreign dancing', well beyond the fold of this new commission.

SLIGO FIDDLE MASTERS IN NEW YORK

When eighteen-year-old Paddy Killoran arrived in New York in 1922, from Ballymote, Co Sligo, the 'Roaring Twenties' were in full swing. By now Irish traditional music had become a performance art, to be listened to in concert halls or at home on new Victrola discs. There was also a thriving Irish dance scene to absorb the newcomer, with a fiddle and a healthy store of tunes, in search of work. The city was rife with small recording companies, like Celtic, Emerald, Gaelic and New Republic, who were making records for local distribution. As the market burgeoned, larger companies like Columbia and Victor started to produce in larger quantities and soon forced the smaller labels out of the market. Killoran's arrival into this bustling scene completed the famed triumvirate of Sligo fiddlers, made up of Michael Coleman and James Morrison and himself, who were to dominate the course of Irish traditional music for the next half century.

Michael Coleman (1891-1945) was born into a small farming community in Knockgrania near Kilavil in Co Sligo. As a young fiddler, he played for house dances in south Sligo and was influenced by the fiddling of John Dowd, whose name appears on several of Coleman's records. In 1914 Coleman emigrated to New York and quickly made the transition from the house dance to the professional concert stage. For the next thirty years, his dynamic fiddling thrived in the opulent nexus of Irish pubs, dance halls and recording studios which flourished in the boom of the 1920s but collapsed into the mire of the Great Depression a decade afterwards. He began his recording career in the spring of 1920 with two sides made for the Shannon and Metro labels. Coleman's virtuoso fiddling was fluid, highly ornamented and fast. It was also marked by a rare ability to reshape old tunes into well-crafted masterpieces. The dance quality of his south Sligo style is particularly obvious in reels like 'Bonnie Kate', 'Jenny's Chickens', 'Tarbolton' and 'The Sailor's Bonnet'. One of the distinguishing characteristics of his recordings is the insensitive piano accompaniment. While some pianists provided basic unobtrusive backing, others were ignorant of modal harmony and Irish dance rhythms and, according to ethnomusicologist Philippe Varlet, 'did their inept best to sabotage otherwise superb performances'.

James Morrison (1893-1947) grew up in a small farming community near Collooney in south Sligo, not far from Michael Coleman's home in Knockgrania. He arrived in the United States in the early 1920s when the emerging recording industry was hunting for talent in Irish clubs and dance halls. Entering the professional fray, his successful recording career lasted from 1921 to 1936. Unlike Coleman, Morrison's style had a marked swing and drive, and was distinguished by short bow strokes and sharp articulation. The piano and guitar accompaniment on some of his recordings creates a rhythmic swing reminiscent of jazz ensembles in the 1930s. Among his most celebrated melodies are 'Paddy on the Turnpike', 'The Dublin Reel' and 'Miss Thornton'. The first is known in Ireland as 'The Bunch of Keys'.

Paddy Killoran (1904-1965) was a native of Emlagation, near Ballymote, Co Sligo. His career as a professional fiddler took him through countless dance halls and Irish clubs in New York City during the 1920s. At one point, he owned a bar in the Bronx. In the 1930s he played with the Pride of Erin Orchestra on board passenger ships travelling to and from Ireland. He began his recording career with the Crown company in 1931 and later recorded for the American branch of Decca. Killoran made numerous solo recordings, as well as duets with his fellow county man Paddy Sweeney, and group recordings with his Pride of Erin Orchestra, a popular dance ensemble which included saxophones and clarinets in its line-up. Killoran's style, with its characteristic simple ornamentation and drive, was ideally suited to dancing. His exemplary settings of 'The Scotchman over the Border', derived from a seventeenth-century march, and 'The Tenpenny Bit', are still popular among traditional fiddlers.

In the United States, the recordings of Coleman, Morrison and Killoran encouraged musicians like James 'Lad' O'Beirne, Louis Quinn, Hughie Gillespie, Ed Reavy, John McKenna and Tom Morrison to follow in their footsteps. In Ireland, thousands of their recordings were consumed with a fervour previously reserved only for Francis O'Neill's *1001*. The sale of American records was so successful in rural Ireland that O'Byrne de Witt's salesman Jer O'Donovan from Glandore, Co Cork, made over twenty trips across the North Atlantic before the outbreak of World War II – years before the arrival of passenger aviation.

The recordings of the Sligo fiddle masters set high standards for aspiring traditional players. In rural areas where regional dialects and repertoires prevailed, the music of Coleman and Morrison became a new imperative. Their techniques and ornamentation, settings and repertoire, were imitated to the finest detail, while local tunes and settings were consigned to the elderly and the uncompromising. The movement towards standardisation which began with O'Neill's book now took another quantum leap ahead. In the ensuing foray, reels took pride of place over jigs and hornpipes, while polkas, slides, mazurkas, highlands and set pieces slipped further into oblivion. By the 1940s it had become commonplace to play the 'American' versions of tunes in the order they were played by Coleman and Morrison on the original 78rpm recordings. Hence, 'Bonnie Kate' was played with 'Jenny's Chickens' while 'Tarbolton' was invariably followed by 'The Longford Collector' and 'The Sailor's Bonnet'.

'COMELY MAIDENS' AND THE DANCE HALLS ACT

The Wall Street Crash in 1929 was followed by the traumatic onslaught of the Great Depression. As savings and investments vanished into thin air, food queues and human despair filled the once-thriving centres of American industry. Musicians who had prospered in the dance hall and on the concert stage now withdrew to the 'speak easy' and the ghetto. The famed as well as the unknown, each in their own way, were badly affected by the collapse of Wall Street. Clare exiles Gret Hegarty and Bridget Donnellan reconciled themselves to the plight of their menfolk, and played concertina music for 'kitchen rackets' in Springfield, Massachusetts. Three thousand miles away their female contemporaries, Molly Carthy and Nora Coughlan in west Clare, also anonymous kitchen players, were already bracing themselves for the onset of a different catastrophe, Ireland's economic war with Britain.

By 1932 Eamon de Valera had severed his connection with the anti-treaty IRA, formed the Fianna Fáil party, and won 72 out of 153 seats in Dáil Eireann. Having set up a government with the help of the Labour Party, Fianna Fáil went on to dominate Irish politics for almost forty years. On arriving in office, de Valera quickly abolished the oath of allegiance to the English monarchy and loosened other ties with the United Kingdom. His lieutenant Seán Lemass, Minister for Industry and Commerce, initiated a series of protectionist policies which helped to develop the Irish economy. State-sponsored bodies like Aer Lingus, CIE and Bord na Móna (the Irish Peat Board) were set up. When the new government withheld the land annuities – loan repayments by Irish farmers to their former British landlords – Britain retaliated by imposing heavy import duties on Irish goods. This economic war continued until 1938 when de Valera agreed to pay £10 million to settle the annuities issue. Britain then returned the last Irish ports to the jurisdiction of the Free State.

The economic war was a time of extreme hardship in rural Ireland. In 1932 over 7,000 immigrants returned to Ireland from depressed economies in Britain and America. By 1937 emigration out of Ireland had reached a staggering 26,000. Most of the new exiles were the offspring of small farmers who had met the full brunt of Britain's embargo. The cattle trade was seriously disrupted and calf prices slumped. While the government introduced compulsory tillage and farm subsidies to relieve the burden, the Irish consumer paid the bill through higher taxation and soaring prices. In the resulting exodus from stagnant farms and working-class homes, hundreds of musicians, singers and dancers left the country.

Those who remained at home had to cope with the contradictions of de Valera's Ireland, a land of economic austerity which, in his own telling words 'would be the home of a people who valued material wealth only as a basis of right living, of a people who were satisfied with frugal comfort and devoted their leisure time to the things of the spirit; a land whose countryside would be joyous with the sounds of industry, the romping of sturdy children, the contests of athletic youth, the laughter of comely maidens'. Despite his romantic craving for a 'traditional' frugal Ireland, de Valera's early years in power were marked by an atmosphere of repressive puritanism. This was particularly endemic in his treatment of modern cinema, jazz music, art and literature. It was also evident in his attempts to control public dancing. Having been reminded by the Gaelic League that 'Our Minister of Finance (responsible for broadcasting) has a soul buried in jazz and is selling the musical soul of the nation,' the Fianna Fáil government passed the Public Dance Halls Act in 1935. A draconian attempt to control public morality, this act banned country house dances, as well as all-night jazz dancing in unlicensed halls. Crossroad dances also came under its hammer. Illegal assemblies of dancers and musicians now had to answer to a formidable trinity of clergy, police and judiciary. In the resulting purge, many musicians and set dancers were silenced, while others defied the system. Oral history in rural areas still recalls house dances being broken up by angry parish priests, sometimes accompanied by members of the police.

Referring to the impact of the act in west Clare, folk composer Junior Crehan recalled that 'the clergy and the politicians abolished the country house dances. They believed that there was immoral conduct carried out at the country houses and that there were no sanitary

111

arrangements. You had to pay three pence tax to the shilling going into the hall which meant money to the government. Where money was charged at the house dance, the government was afraid the money was going to an illegal organisation. That put an end to the country house. The country house was our school where we learned to play music and dance. And it was a crying shame it was closed down against the country people. 'Twas our hands raised the walls of these cabins, where our children were born and bred, where our weddings and christenings were merry, where we watched and keened over our dead.'

As young people left the flagstone kitchens for the parish halls, the céilí bands flourished. The building of village halls, usually managed by parish priests, in the decades following the Dance Halls Act, led to the formation of new céilí bands. By the mid-1930s the Kilfenora Céilí Band, which had emerged from a fife-and-drum background in the 1890s, started to play for 'supervised' dances in schools and village halls throughout north Clare and south Galway. Other céilí bands followed their example, among them the Tulla, the Fiach Roe, the Fergus, the Laichtín Naofa and the Belharbour. One of the most coveted honours for a céilí band in the 1930s and 1940s was to broadcast live from Radio Eireann. While this novelty gave a renewed sense of status to traditional performers, especially in their own communities, it also subjected them to pompous standards of musical literacy, which became endemic in 2RN after the appointment, in 1935, of Dr TJ Kiernan as director. From now on, Irish music broadcasts began to move away from the traditional céilí house to the 'respectable' high culture of the concert hall and the Radio Éireann Light Orchestra, which arrived on the scene in the early 1940s. In the wake of these changes, traditional musicians had to be 'auditioned' and screened by a caste of classical music directors before broadcasting to the nation – a practice which survived in Radio Éireann down to the 1950s.

Despite the dramatic upheavals of the 1930s, some unique pockets of traditional music survived, especially in parts of rural Sligo, Leitrim, Galway, Clare and Kerry. It was to these areas and to their old rituals of wrenboys, strawboys, *swarees*, and *cuairding* houses that the Irish Folklore Commission sent its collectors in the 1940s. Growing out of the Irish Folklore Society and the Irish Folklore Institute, the Folklore Commission was set up in 1935. As the spectre of world war approached, the new commission made an eleventh-hour sprint to save Ireland's rich reserve of folklore and songs from oblivion.

PROFILE: JOHNNY DORAN: TRAVELLING PIPER

'With the lengthening of the days and the coming of the hawthorn blossom and the mayfly, Johnny Doran's gaily-coloured horse-drawn caravan could be seen drifting lazily towards a sheep fair in Kilrush, or a house dance in Quilty.' This was how the writer PJ Curtis described the renowned piper Johnny Doran, who travelled the roads of the West of Ireland in the 1930s and 1940s.

Doran was born in 1907 into a family of itinerant pipers who were related to the legendary Wicklow piper John Cash. When he was in his twenties, Doran took to the road in a horse-drawn caravan and continued a family tradition that spanned generations of Dorans in south Leinster. For the next twenty years, his travels took him from Wicklow and Wexford to Sligo, Mayo and Cavan. His favourite counties were, by his own admission, Clare and Galway, where traditional music was still vibrant, and respect for the travelling piper implicit in the mindset of many rural communities. An unlikely combination of piping and horse trading earned him a comfortable living at a time when most of his rural patrons were experiencing economic hardship. Doran's dynamic piping could be heard at various public gatherings, from hurling matches and horse shows to fair days and sports meetings. His music had a unique charismatic quality, and stories are still told about its exhilarating impact on market-day audiences. One young witness in the 1940s recalled seeing mountainy farmers, clad in hob-nailed boots and tweed caps, break into wild bouts of solo dancing on hearing Doran's music. His piping also won the attention of enthusiastic pupils, among them Willie Clancy and Martin Talty of Milltown Malbay. Through Doran's inspiration, Clare's piping tradition, which had been broken since the death of Garrett Barry in 1899, was restored in the 1940s by pipers like Seán Reid, Willie Clancy, Martin Talty, Michael Falsey and Martin Rocheford.

Unlike his domesticated peers, Doran played mainly out of doors in a standing position, with his leg placed on a T-shaped rest. His legato, open style of piping reached its zenith in classic pieces like 'Rakish Paddy', 'Colonel Fraser', 'The Steam Packet' and 'The Coppers and Brass'. These were among the tunes he recorded for Kevin Danaher from the Folklore Commission in 1946. Two years later, a wall fell on Doran's caravan while it was parked near Christchurch, Dublin. He never recovered from the accident and died, aged forty-three, in January 1950. He was buried in Rathnew, Co Wicklow. His piping influenced the piping of Dubliner Paddy Keenan, who continues to play many of Doran's classic dance tunes today.

ENNIS, Ó RIADA AND THE FLEADH:
A TRADITION RESTORED

When World War II broke out in September 1939, the Irish Free State opted to remain neutral, despite the misgivings of its island neighbours. The period from 1939 to 1945 was referred to officially as the 'Emergency'. It was a time of social vigilance and fastidious censorship, as local defence forces readied themselves for the possibility of invasion and the Free State government rationed essential food supplies and fuel. Despite the prolonged foreboding however, Ireland was never of sufficient importance for either side to invade. Apart from a verbal fracas between Winston Churchill and Éamon de Valera, and a mistaken attack on Dublin's northside by the German Luftwaffe, the war passed without any serious infringement on Ireland.

With the ending of the Emergency, the Irish public was ready for a change of government. De Valera called a general election in February 1948, a move which saw the ousting of his Fianna Fáil government for the first time since 1932. The new Inter-Party government which came into office was an uneasy coalition led by John A Costello. By the end of the year, this coalition passed the Republic of Ireland Act and withdrew the country officially from the British Commonwealth. Despite its initial novelty, the Inter-Party government proved incapable of stemming the increasing tide of emigration from rural Ireland which followed in the wake of the war. The government collapsed in 1951 in the face of clerical opposition to Dr Noel Browne's 'Mother and Child Scheme', a scheme advocating free medical treatment for expectant mothers, which was seen by Catholic bishops as an infringement on the rights of the family.

The traditional musician remained as susceptible to the ebb and flow of the Irish economy as any of his contemporaries. Only inheriting males could enjoy any modicum of certainty in rural Ireland. Non-inheriting females, as well as the working-classes in small towns and cities, continued to emigrate throughout the 1940s. During the wartime boom in British industry, many found work in munitions factories in Coventry and other Midland cities. Irish navvies and construction workers found plenty of employment rebuilding London after Hitler's bombing blitz. Irish immigrants in wartime London could dance three nights a week at the Tara Club on Brixton Road where Frank Lee and his Radio and Recording Tara Céilí Band played a lively mix of Irish and 'modern' dances.

MUSIC AND DANCING IN WARTIME DUBLIN

While England claimed the lion's share of Irish emigrants, Dublin too attracted its quota of migrant workers, among them musicians who deserted rural Ireland during the 'Hungry Forties'. Pipers and fiddlers became so numerous in Dublin during the Emergency that the Dublin Pipers' Club, which had been defunct since 1926, was successfully revived in 1940 by Leo Rowsome, Seán Reid and Tommy Reck. Its home in Thomas Street became a meeting place for traditional musicians from all over Ireland.

Céilí dancing also enjoyed a high profile in wartime Dublin. Céilithe were held regularly in the Mansion House and an annual dress céilí was held in the State Apartments of Dublin Castle on St Patrick's Night. Among the most popular céilí bands of the day was the Kincora, led by Sligo fiddler Kathleen Harrington, and the Dublin Metropolitan Garda Céilí Band, comprised of rural migrants like Joe Liddy, who left Dromahair, Co Leitrim, in the early 1930s to join the police force in Dublin.

The Potts family, originally from Wexford, was one of Dublin's most revered musical families in the 1940s. John Potts was an authority on the uilleann pipes and his sons, Tommy and Eddie, played fiddle and pipes. While Eddie won major accolades at the Dublin *Feis Ceoil* on fiddle and pipes, his brother Tommy went on to become one of Ireland's foremost 'soul' fiddlers whose enigmatic style, off-beat rhythms and improvisation transcended the dance music tradition of the time. Throughout the 1930s and 1940s, John Potts's house in Crumlin became an 'academy' of piping and fiddling. Among his pupils were pipers Tommy Reck, whose family also came from Wexford, Seán Reid, a native of Castlefin, Co Donegal, and Breandán Breathnach from Dublin. All three were to play seminal roles in the revival of Irish piping during the next four decades, and Breathnach was to become a distinguished collector and authority on Irish traditional music.

COLLECTORS AND BROADCASTERS

One of the most prolific collectors and broadcasters of Irish traditional music in the 1940s was the piper Séamus Ennis. A native of the Naul in north county Dublin, Séamus received his early training in music transcription from his father James and, later on, from music publisher Colm Ó Lochlainn at The Sign of the Three Candles press in Dublin. Séamus worked with Ó Lochlainn, who published a popular series of *Irish Street Ballads,* from 1938 to 1942. However, as wartime shortages restricted printing operations, Ennis considered moving to London to join the Royal Air Force. Horrified by such a prospect, Ó Lochlainn arranged for him to meet Séamus Delargy, founder and director of the Irish Folklore Commission. In 1942, at the age of twenty-three, Ennis began his first collecting assignment for the Commission in Cois Fharraige, the Aran Islands, and further west in Carna, where he met Colm Ó Caoidheáin from Glinsk, one of the Connemara's most revered *sean nós* singers.

Séamus Ennis was eminently qualified as a collector. A master piper and an accomplished singer, he had an excellent knowledge of Irish dialects, and had received a thorough training in music notation during his apprenticeship. He also had a razor-sharp ear, a prodigious memory, and an uncanny ability to reproduce tunes and songs on first hearing. Unlike later collectors, Ennis had no mechanical recording equipment. His only tools were a pen, a satchel of music sheets and a tin whistle to verify his transcriptions. From 1942 to 1947 he travelled throughout the West of Ireland on a bicycle, returning to Dublin to write up his notes, transcribe tunes and deposit his material in the folklore archive. As well as collecting in Connemara, Cork, Kerry and Donegal, he spent an extended period collecting music on the Hebrides off the west coast of Scotland.

When Ennis left the Commission after a five-year term he had collected over 2,000 pieces, between songs and dance tunes, an achievement unsurpassed by any of his predecessors in the field. He continued his work as a collector with Radio Eireann from 1947 to 1951. Unlike the materials collected for the Commission, the music Ennis and his colleagues Proinsias Ó Conluain and Seán Mac Réamoinn collected for Radio Eireann was intended for broadcast. Hence a greater emphasis was placed on dance tunes. Among Ennis's chief sources were the Dohertys and the O'Beirnes from Donegal, the Russells and Willie Clancy from Clare and the celebrated Pádraig O'Keefe from Sliabh Luachra. Ennis recalled one such meeting with O'Keefe, in Lyon's public house in Scartaglin. When the ritual chat had been dispensed with and O'Keefe was ready for his third pint, he pulled a sheaf of music from his pocket. Surprised to see that O'Keefe had written out the tunes himself, Ennis thanked him and reminded him that he should not have gone to the bother, as he was paid to transcribe the music. *'Th'anam an diabhail,'* replied O'Keefe, 'isn't it better than wasting good drinking time while you're writing them and "Scart" open.'

The BBC began collecting traditional music in Ireland during the summer of 1947. This project was initiated by radio producer Brian George. Collectors Seán Ó Baoil and Peter Kennedy in the north of Ireland recorded rural- and urban-based performers, among them Irish and English singers, fiddlers, pipers, flute players and accordionists. In 1951 Séamus Ennis joined the BBC and, during the next seven years, helped build up a mammoth store of field recordings from all over Ireland, England and Scotland. Most of these recordings, which amount to 1,500 performances, were broadcast on the popular BBC radio programme 'As I Roved Out'. The archive materials collected by Ennis and his colleagues during this prolific period represent an unprecedented achievement in the documentation of Irish traditional music.

While certain parts of Ireland were too remote to pick up the BBC's 'As I Roved Out', Ciarán Mac Mathúna's *'Ceolta Tíre'* and 'Job of Journeywork' were winning huge audiences all over Ireland by the mid-1950s. A native of Limerick, Mac Mathúna studied Comparative Folklore at University College, Dublin. In 1955 he began presenting traditional music programmes on Radio Éireann and travelled extensively throughout the West of Ireland collecting music, folklore and song. With the assistance of a mobile recording unit, he managed to tape traditional musicians in their own localities. His recording sessions, which were conducted in country kitchens, public houses and small halls, reflected the natural milieu of the musician in a manner which was far more authentic than studio or concert hall recordings. Not only did his programmes create a discerning forum for musicians and singers, but they also created an urban audience for what was essentially a rural art form. His work as a collector and broadcaster also took him to the United States and Canada in 1962 and 1966 where he recorded celebrated figures like accordionist Joe Cooley, fiddlers Larry Redigan, Martin Wynne and Johnny Cronin and piper Tomás Standevin.

IRISH MUSIC IN NEW YORK AND LONDON

America during the 1950s contrasted radically with the frugal world that many traditional musicians left behind them in rural Ireland. American industry was galloping through a huge post-war boom, Hollywood was churning out its big-screen icons, and a well of opportunities awaited the work-hungry immigrant. The audience for Irish traditional music however had changed considerably since the halcyon days of Coleman and Morrison in the 1920s. By now, 'Bonnie Kate' had well and truly ceded her place to 'Danny Boy', while most Irish-Americans were delighted to be entertained by the sugar-coated shenanigans of Mickey Rooney and Bing Crosby. In the 1950s and 1960s several attempts were made to 'legitimise' the status of Irish traditional music by placing it on a par with high art music. The United Irish Counties Association held an annual *feis* in New York, which endeavoured to equate the folk arts with the high arts. Musicians entering competitions in this intriguing event were required to play classical pieces from composers like Bach and Mozart as well as classical arrangements of Irish tunes.

The steady influx of immigrant musicians helped to sustain Irish traditional music in New York in the 1950s. The period saw the arrival of celebrated accordionists Joe Cooley from Peterswell, Co Galway, and Paddy O'Brien from the Lough Derg village of Portroe in north Tipperary. East Galway flute player Jack Coen also found work in New York City, where he still enjoys considerable prominence. He was followed shortly afterwards by his brother, Fr Charlie Coen, who brought the concertina music of Connie Hogan from Woodford to the States. Kerry fiddlers Johnny and Paddy Cronin, as well as Longford fiddler Paddy Reynolds, had also made their way to America by the 1950s. In fact, Johnny Cronin, Joe Cooley and Paddy O'Brien shared the same apartment block in the Bronx for a brief period. Composer Martin

Mulhaire got his first taste of the United States while touring with the Tulla Céilí Band, and failed to return home with his colleagues. He was joined in New York shortly afterwards by flute player Mike Preston who also played with the Tulla Céilí Band during its heydays of the 1950s.

Immigrant musicians performed at *feiseanna,* picnics, concerts and céilí gatherings, as well as in Irish bars and house sessions all over New York. Music work was sufficiently plentiful to prompt the formation of the New York Céilí Band in the 1950s. This illustrious ensemble included masters like Andy McGann and Paddy Reynolds on fiddle, accordionist Paddy O'Brien, flute player Jack Coen, and Felix Dolan on piano. Bookings for groups like the New York Céilí Band came from all over the city, as well as from Irish holiday villages in the Catskills, which attracted hordes of musicians, singers and dancers during the summer months (before cheap air travel ferried them back to 'the old country' during the 1970s). Although Sligo music was popularised in New York by flute player Mike Flynn, who recorded with Paddy Killoran, and fiddlers Andy McGann (a student of Coleman), Lad O'Beirne and the composer Martin Wynne, master flute players Jack Coen, Mike Rafferty and Mike McHale ensured the presence of an equally rich store of music from east Galway and Roscommon. The dual presence of Sligo and east Galway dialects still distinguishes the music-making of New York City today.

London, too, received its quota of immigrant musicians in the early 1950s, although the host culture was somewhat less receptive than its New York counterpart. Popular opinion in England was still resentful of the fact that Ireland had remained neutral during World War II, and saw the immigrant Irish as opportunists, reaping the benefits of post-war prosperity. For the immigrant, however, Irish traditional music acted as a welcome antidote to the pressures of an inhospitable cockney environment. After a week spent on a construction site, or battling with bedrock in a man-hole beneath the street, hordes of Irish workers thronged the Irish pubs in Camden Town, Cricklewood and Kilburn High Road on Friday evenings. Here the musicians, who shared their fate during the working week, offered them an occasion to renew their sense of community, before MacAlpine marshalled them to work again on Monday morning. Pubs like the Eagle in Camden Town, the Bedford Arms, the Fulham Broadway and the Crown in Cricklewood, all rang with the sounds of Irish music sessions. Their roster of house musicians reads like a litany of Irish music icons – fiddlers Bobby Casey and Joe Ryan from Clare, *sean nós* singer Joe Heaney and fiddler Máirtín Byrnes from Galway, flute player Roger Sherlock and fiddler Michael Gorman from Sligo and pipers Willie Clancy and Tommy McCarthy from Clare. Their sessions went on to attract renowned players like Paddy Breen, Danny Meehan, Brendan McGlinchey, John Bowe, Kieran Collins, Des Donnelly, Raymond Roland, Liam Farrell, PJ Crotty, Mick O'Connor and Brendan Mulkere. The céilí band also enjoyed a popular profile in contemporary London, not least at the Galtymore in Cricklewood and the Irish Centre in Camden Square. Among the best-known céilí bands of the period were the Dunloe Céilí Band and the Four Courts Céilí Band, which included fiddler Lucy Farr from Ballinakill, Co Galway, and flute player Paddy Taylor from Co Limerick.

THE FLEADH CHEOIL MOVEMENT

In the socially polarised Ireland of the 1940s, the status afforded to the traditional musician was well beneath that accorded to his 'high art' counterpart. Shunned by the educational establishment, ignored by the popular press, and derided by urban music societies, many traditional performers had a low self-image of their role in Irish music and of its place in contemporary Ireland. Those who ventured into the competitive domain of the *feis ceoil* were often met with the retort that they should 'learn to play properly' before presenting themselves again to 'informed' adjudicators. By the early 1950s, moves were afoot to stem this process of denigration and create an all-encompassing forum to raise the morale of traditional performers.

In January 1951 members of the Dublin Pipers' Club travelled to Mullingar to help set up a pipers' club in the Westmeath capital. After a lengthy meeting, the visitors and their hosts decided to set up an organisation which would embrace all traditional instruments. A second meeting was held one month later, during which it was decided to organise a *fleadh cheoil* on Whit weekend, in conjunction with the Midlands *feis* in Mullingar. The group, which was to style itself Cumann Ceoltóirí na hEireann, included Cáit Bean Uí Mhuineacháin, Leo and Tom Rowsome, Paddy McElvanny, Jim Seery and Eamon Ó Muineacháin. They issued invitations to traditional musicians from all over Ireland to attend their Whit weekend gathering. The festival proved to be a phenomenal success. Starting in Mullingar with a small core of musicians, many of them students of Leo Rowsome from the Municipal School of Music in Dublin, the *fleadh cheoil* burgeoned into a dynamic new forum for musicians, singers and dancers.

By 1956, the *fleadh cheoil*, which was held that year in Ennis, Co Clare, had become a national event, with parades and pageants, street sessions and music competitions. In fulfilling the aims of its founders, who had now changed their name to Comhaltas Ceoltóirí Éireann, the annual event was now attracting a myriad of legendary performers – Willie Clancy, Elizabeth Crotty, Paddy Canny, Aggie White, Peter O'Loughlin, Paddy Murphy, Paddy Carthy, and countless others – who left an indelible imprint on Irish traditional music in the 1950s and 1960s. The climax of the *fleadh* was the All-Ireland Céilí Band Competition. Rallying support with the parochial vigour of hurling teams and political parties, céilí bands like the Kilfenora and the Tulla, the Laichtín Naofa and the Fiach Roe competed enthusiastically for the Dal gCais Shield, the most acknowledged symbol of competitive success in the Comhaltas calendar.

While the *fleadh cheoil* gave traditional musicians a new platform and an appreciative audience, it also increased the emphasis on competitive playing. Despite its debilitating impact on regional styles, this competitive nexus was expanded in the 1960s to include county and provincial arenas. *Fleadh Cheoil na hÉireann* has flourished as a global crossroads for traditional musicians, singers and dancers. Four decades after its tentative birth in Mullingar, it has become a premier event in Ireland's musical calendar. One of its unique features is the annual influx of performers from Britain and North America. Soloists like Kathleen Collins, Billy McComiskey, Joanie Madden, Brian Conway and Liz Carroll have represented the North American chapters of Comhaltas over the years, while celebrated céilí bands like the Liverpool, The Thatch and St Colmcilles have raised their standards on behalf of the Irish in Britain.

SEÁN Ó RIADA AND CEOLTÓIRÍ CHUALANN

Although the *fleadh cheoil* movement and the seminal broadcasts of Ciarán Mac Mathúna raised the morale of musicians in the 1950s, few could have anticipated the phenomenal influence of Seán Ó Riada, who transformed the status of Irish traditional music in the 1960s. According to his friend, the poet Thomas Kinsella, Ó Riada 'reached out and swiftly captured a national audience, lifted the level of musical practice and appreciation, restored to his people an entire cultural dimension, and added no little to the gaiety of the nation'.

Seán Ó Riada was born in Cork in 1931 and brought up in Bruff, a small market town in Co Limerick. He learned to play the traditional fiddle while growing up in Limerick and returned eventually to Cork to study music under Professor Aloys Fleischmann. On graduating from University College Cork with a degree in music in 1952 he was appointed Assistant Director of Music in Radio Eireann. Less than two years later he resigned from Radio Eireann to study music in France and Italy, where he was influenced by the compositions of Schoenberg. On returning to Ireland he was appointed Music Director of the Abbey Theatre, a post which he held for the next seven years. In 1963, he took up an academic position at UCC. Shortly afterwards he moved, with his family, to the Irish-speaking village of Cúil Aodha in west Cork where he lived until his untimely death in 1971.

Ó Riada's career as a classical composer spanned the period 1957 to 1965, and included works like *Hercules Dux Ferrariae* (Nomos No. 1) and *Five Greek Epigrams* (Nomos No. 2). He also composed a number of liturgical works, which are still performed regularly by the Irish-language choir he founded in Cúil Aodha. His rise to national prominence, however, came through his film scores. In 1960 Gael Linn, the Irish Language Organisation, invited him to compose the score for George Morrison's documentary film, *Mise Eire,* which portrayed the events leading up to the foundation of the state. The public reaction to the film was phenomenal and Ó Riada immediately became a national celebrity. Another score followed in 1961, this time for a film version of *The Playboy of the Western World* featuring Abbey actress Siobhán McKenna. This project featured the music of Ceoltóirí Chualann, a traditional ensemble which Ó Riada had put together in 1960. The group, which comprised of Dublin-born, as well as Dublin-based musicians from the West of Ireland, included fiddlers John Kelly, Seán Keane and Martin Fay, piper Paddy Moloney, flute player Michael Tubridy, accordionists Sonny Brogan and Éamon de Buitléar, singers Darach Ó Catháin and Seán Ó Sé, and Ronnie McShane on bones. Ó Riada himself played the *bodhrán* and harpsichord, and claimed that the latter was more closely related to the mediaeval Irish *cruit* than the neo-Irish harp, which was then being touted by the Irish tourist industry. Throughout the 1960s, the dynamic new sound of Ceoltóirí Chualann and the authoritative exuberance of Ó Riada took Irish traditional music into a 'brave new world', away from the country house session and into the 'high art' concert halls of the nation.

Using traditional instruments, Ó Riada introduced his chamber ensemble to classical-style arrangements, harmonies, improvisation, and dress suits – all of which helped to place their rural art on a par with other 'socially correct' art forms in urban Ireland. His 'new departure' interspersed solos, duets and trios with the full ensemble sound, and became a benchmark for the next generation of traditional performers. Ceoltóirí Chualann made their first public appearance in the Abbey Theatre where they played for Bryan MacMahon's play *The Golden Folk*. The next four years involved little or no concert work. Instead, the group became known to the nation through two series of radio programmes, *'Reacaireacht an Riadaigh'* and *'Fleadh Cheoil an Raidió'*. As well as highlighting the *sean nós* song tradition, Ó Riada was anxious to revive the compositions of the eighteenth-century harpers, especially the work of O'Carolan. Consequently, the repertoire of Ceoltóirí Chualann included pieces like 'Planxty O'Rourke', 'O'Carolan's Concerto' and 'Planxty Davis', which had enjoyed little or no standing among traditional performers prior to the 1960s. Ceoltóirí Chualann ceased to perform regularly after Ó Riada moved to Cúil Aodha. Their final recordings were made live at the Gaiety Theatre in Dublin in March 1969. The occasion was a concert to commemorate the bicentenary of the Gaelic poet Peadar Ó Doirnín. The recordings issued by Gael Linn were simply titled *Ó Riada sa Gaiety* and *Ó Riada*. The first contained *'Mná na hEireann'*, composed by Ó Riada to the original poem by Ó Doirnín.

Apart from creating a popular audience for traditional music, Ó Riada was also an inspiring educator. This was especially obvious in his series 'Our Musical Heritage', which he broadcast on Radio Éireann in 1962. Delivered in his own emphatic style, his talks made musicians more aware of their art, its rich historical background, and its technical diversity. The series also created a framework within which traditional music could be assessed by its practitioners and its enthusiasts. Understandably, some of Ó Riada's blunt opinions provoked the ire of his audience. For example, he likened céilí music to the buzzing of a bluebottle in an upturned jamjar, a comparison which failed to impress many listeners in Clare where céilí bands had enjoyed major cultural prominence since the early 1900s.

THE BOOMING SIXTIES: JIVES AND LOUNGE BARS

Throughout the 1960s, rural as well as urban Ireland underwent a pivotal series of social and economic changes. The Lemass-Whitaker Economic Plan, introduced in the 1950s, dislodged the country from its insular moorings, boosted native industry and opened the floodgates to foreign investment. With the first signs of economic prosperity, emigrants returned home in droves. In the resulting transition, new schools and housing estates were built, families became more affluent, and the lounge bar replaced the public house, that select bastion of the Irish male. A modern consumerism replaced the frugal conservatism of an older era. The newly-established RTE television service swept into homes and bars all over the country. Small shopkeepers hastened to upgrade, ageing snugs and beer-stained counters gave way to neon lights and plastic fittings, while John Hinde postcards portrayed an Ireland of pristine vistas and holiday havens. Once the sanctuary of the blacksmith's anvil and the squinting window of the gossipmonger, rural villages now catered for busloads of wealthy tourists and foreign motor cars. In the midst of all these changes, the Second Vatican Council helped to take the autocratic sting out of Irish Catholicism.

Musicians had an integral part to play in this new consumer-oriented Ireland. Unlike their predecessors, who played in kitchens and village halls, traditional musicians in the 1960s chose, for the first time, to play 'professionally' in lounge bars. These had now opened their doors to women, and had taken on the function of community centres in many rural communities. In this environment the musician became a paid employee, and his entertainment a vital prerequisite in the profit-based relationship between patron and publican. As musicians left céilí bands to play in lounge bars, they formed trios and quartets, comprised typically of a singer, guitarist, drummer and accordionist. Their repertoires also changed: while céilí band audiences danced mainly to reels, jigs and hornpipes, lounge bar patrons had more eclectic tastes. By the mid-1960s, imported country-and-western music had become standard fare. Lounge-bar musicians churned out jives and jigs, waltzes and quick steps, interspersed with popular ballads, which were then enjoying a major media boom on both sides of the Atlantic.

Television had been a vital factor in sparking the ballad boom in the 1960s. Nowhere was this more evident than in the United States where the Clancy Brothers and Tommy Makem had created a phenomenal audience for Irish ballads. Tom, Paddy and Liam Clancy had emigrated from south Tipperary in the 1950s. By the end of the decade, they found themselves singing Irish ballads in

New York's Greenwich Village, where the folk revival was in full swing. Surrounded by legendary figures like Peter, Paul and Mary, Bob Dylan, Pete Seeger and Joan Baez, Tommy Makem, from Co Armagh, and the Clancys sang their ballads with a gusto that was seldom heard on the American stage. A sixteen-minute spot on the celebrated Ed Sullivan TV show in 1961 made them overnight sensations with audiences all over the US. They went on to perform at Carnegie Hall and eventually crossed the Atlantic to sing at the Royal Albert Hall in London. Their sensational return to Ireland corresponded with the take-off of national television, which gave them access to a new and avid audience. Within days, their street rhyme 'I'll Tell My Ma' was on the lips of every schoolchild in the country.

The recording industry in Ireland was also prospering. During the late 1950s Gael Linn produced a seminal series of 78rpm recordings. These focused on solo performances from fiddlers like Seán Ryan, Denis Murphy, Paddy Canny, the piper Willie Clancy and *sean nós* singer Seán 'ac Dhonncha, all of whom were masters of their traditional crafts. By now, the accordion had taken centre stage in traditional music circles. Companies like HMV found a ready-made market for records of accordion players like Paddy O'Brien and George Ross. The exuberant fiddling of Seán Maguire had also found its way onto disc, alongside recordings of céilí bands like the Tulla and the Kilfenora. The first LP of Irish traditional music was recorded in 1960. Titled simply *All Ireland Champions*, it featured the unique Clare sound of fiddlers Paddy Canny and PJ Hayes, and flute player Peadar O'Loughlin. They were accompanied on piano by Bridie Lafferty. Recorded in two short studio sessions by Shamrock Records Dublin, this LP has now become a collector's item, not least because of its rare dialect of traditional tunes and its unhurried dance rhythm. Smaller companies also emerged onto the marketplace. Breandán Breathnach's *Spól* label produced a superb EP featuring Ballinakill fiddler Aggie White and Kilmaley flute player Peadar O'Loughlin. Although other projects in the series were planned, Breathnach's work as a collector and publisher of traditional music took him in another direction during the 1960s.

Throughout the 1960s, the ballad boom spawned a roof-ripping generation of guitar strummers and spoon tappers, from the brash to the musical, the obscure to the idolised, who poured out their hearts in the so-called 'singing pubs' of the nation. Among the most acclaimed ballad groups to emerge during this period were the Dubliners, the Wolfe Tones, the Johnstons, the Ludlows, the Emmett Spiceland and the Fureys. The 1960s also witnessed the emergence of several new céilí bands, especially in Dublin, despite Ó Riada's tirade against céilí-band music. The most prominent of these were the Lough Gamhna and the Castle Céilí Band. The former, which included Tony MacMahon, Paddy Maloney, Seán Bracken, Owen O'Reilly and Eamon de Buitléar, had its heyday in the early 1960s. The Castle Céilí came to national prominence at *Fleadh Cheoil na hÉireann* and *Oireachtas na Gaeilge* from 1963 onwards. A lively blend of youth and experience, the Castle consisted of Seán and James Keane (fiddle and accordion), John O'Dwyer (fiddle), Mick O'Connor (flute), John Kelly (fiddle), Joe Ryan (fiddle), Michael Tubridy (flute), Bridie Lafferty (piano) and Benny Carey (drums). Paddy O'Brien from Offaly filled the accordion slot in 1969 when James Keane emigrated to America. When not playing formally as a céilí band, members of the Castle could be found playing together at the Church Street Traditional Club and in O'Donoghue's pub in Merrion Row, two of the few Dublin establishments where traditional musicians could escape the onslaught of the ballad boom.

THE CHIEFTAINS: MUSICAL AMBASSADORS

While the break up of Ceoltóirí Chualann in 1969 led to the formation of Ceoltóirí Laighean by Éamon de Buitléar, the Chieftains had emerged as a recording ensemble as early as 1963, with the release of *Chieftains 1*. This recording, which reflected Seán Ó Riada's seminal influence, was meant to be a once-off project. It featured the music of Paddy Maloney on uilleann pipes, Michael Tubridy on flute and concertina, Seán Potts on whistle, Martin Fay on fiddle, and Davey Fallon on *bodhrán*. In the early years, public appearances as the Chieftains were few, and several members of the group played with céilí bands, or as part of Ó Riada's Ceoltóirí Chualann. An invitation to play at the Edinburgh Festival in 1968 brought the group to the attention of a wider European audience. At this point, Dublin fiddler Seán Keane had joined the group and Peadar Mercier had taken over from Davey Fallon.

The Chieftains' first foray into the domain of popular culture came in 1970 when they shared the stage at the National Stadium in Dublin with Fairport Convention. They became a full-time professional outfit in 1975. The personnel of the group continued to change, however, through the 1970s. Belfast harper Derek Bell became a member in 1972. Dublin singer and *bodhrán* player Kevin Conneff took over from Peadar Mercier in 1976, and Seán Potts and Michael Tubridy ceded their places to Roscommon flute player Matt Molloy in 1979.

For over thirty years the Chieftains have played for audiences in North America, Europe and Australia. In 1983 they toured in the Peoples' Republic of China and performed with the Chinese Broadcasting Art Group who played Irish tunes on traditional Chinese instruments like the *Yangqin* and the *Erhu*. The Chieftains have also performed with concert, symphony, and chamber orchestras, and have arranged music for theatre, cinema and ballet. They have been associated with a plethora of rock stars like Dire Straits, The Rolling Stones and Sting. While these affiliations have disturbed many staunch tradition-bearers in Ireland, the film scores generated by the Chieftains have helped to introduce global audiences to Irish traditional music. These began in 1975 with Stanley Kubrick's film *Barry Lyndon*. Other film scores followed, among them *Purple Taxi, Far and Away, The Grey Fox, Circle of Friends* and the more recent *Rob Roy*.

With over thirty commercial recordings, the Chieftains have placed Irish traditional music on a par with other music genres in the world of popular entertainment. Their enterprise has been rewarded by five Grammy Awards in recent years. These include *Another Country*, recorded in Nashville; *The Celtic Harp*, featuring Janet Harbison and the Belfast Harp Orchestra in a tribute to Edward Bunting; and *Santiago*.

PROFILE: SEÁN REID – VISIONARY AND PIPER

The Clare piper Martin Talty once described Seán Reid as 'a gentleman piper and a scholar'. While this description may well prompt an image of old-world antiquarianism, Seán Reid's prolific life as a musician, collector and researcher of Irish traditional music presents a radically different portrait. A pivotal figure in the Irish piping world, Reid's inspiring vision, in-depth knowledge and uncompromising tenacity contributed to a myriad of cultural movements which influenced the course of Irish traditional music from the 1930s to the present day.

Seán Reid was born in Castlefin, Co Donegal, in 1907. On the death of his father, his family moved to Castlederg, Co Tyrone. He learnt to play the fiddle as a child, although his mother had moral doubts about his musical inclinations. He first encountered the uilleann pipes at the Glens *feis* in Cushendun, Co Antrim, in 1930. They were played by RL O'Mealy from Belfast. His interest was further fuelled when he discovered an old 78rpm recording of Chicago piper Tom Ennis. At this point, Seán was an engineering student at Queen's University, Belfast. In 1934 Reid found an engineering job in Dublin and met the fiddler Tommy Potts. Shortly afterwards, Reid became a student of John Potts, one of the foremost piping authorities in Ireland. Reid's commitment to the art of piping brought him into contact with legendary figures like Leo Rowsome, Tommy Reck and Breandán Breathnach – an association which eventually led to the revival of the Dublin Pipers' Club in 1940.

In 1937 Seán Reid was offered a position with the Clare County Council. Shortly after arriving in Clare, he met the travelling piper Johnny Doran and their friendship was to endure until Doran's tragic death in 1950. Reid's journeys to west Clare brought him into contact with pipers Willie Clancy, Martin Talty, Michael Falsey and Peter O'Loughlin and flute player JC Talty. In 1939 he met the east Clare piper Martin Rochford. Throughout the 1940s, Reid promoted the art of piping in Clare, working diligently to locate practice sets of pipes for beginners, and furnish experienced players with full sets. He was also fortunate to own a car in an era when most country people travelled by horse and cart, by bicycle or on foot. His car transported musicians from various parts of rural Clare, to places well beyond the 'walking distances' of their own locales. He also drove his small corps of Clare pipers to the annual Oireachtas gathering in Dublin throughout the 1940s and 1950s.

In 1948, Reid became leader of the Tulla Céilí Band which included musicians from east and west Clare, as well as Aggie White and Joe Cooley from east Galway. In the socially divided Clare of the period, however, Reid's musical activities did not go unnoticed by his superiors in Ennis. They were less than enthusiastic about their civil engineer playing with a céilí band, and meeting 'every Tom, Dick and Harry at the crossroads'. Despite the myopia of his supervisors, Reid carried on doing what he enjoyed most, playing traditional music. In the 1950s he was a key figure in promoting Comhaltas Ceoltóirí Eireann in Clare. Concerned with the future of uilleann piping, he campaigned for the establishment of Na Píobairí Uilleann in Bettystown, Co Meath, in 1968. Despite the misgivings of Comhaltas Ceoltóirí Eireann, who felt that the piping revival should be nurtured within its own organisation, Na Píobairí Uilleann has gone on to safeguard the status of Irish piping, encourage the manufacture of uilleann pipes, establish an extensive archive centre in Henrietta Street in Dublin and build a network of branches all over the world. One of its main events is the Willie Clancy Summer School which meets every July in Milltown Malbay, Co Clare. Reid was one of the primary architects of this international forum, which celebrated twenty-five years of successful teaching in 1997. His astute diplomatic ability was also a vital factor in forging a cross-border alliance between musicians in the Republic of Ireland and their northern counterparts in the Antrim and Derry Fiddlers' Association.

FROM FRIEL'S KITCHEN TO THE NEW MILLENNIUM

By the 1970s, Ireland had undergone a rapid series of pivotal changes. The self-conscious nativism of the 1940s had given way to an emergent pluralism, urbanisation and industrialisation. Ireland's entry into the European Economic Community was followed by a welcome boost in regional development, improved educational standards and new levels of Irish tourism. By then, the youth of the nation was also being absorbed into the mainstream of American popular culture.

The arts too fared well in this cosmopolitan

mid-Atlantic milieu. In 1973 the Arts Council of Ireland was restructured, and in 1980, Dublin fiddler Paddy Glackin was appointed to the new position of Traditional Music Officer with the Council. His brief was to monitor and develop policies which would impact the preservation and performance of traditional music. By this time, however, traditional musicians were being swept along by the inexorable currents of social and economic change which were altering the course of Irish life.

As musicians pondered their new-found notoriety in the 1970s and 1980s, it became self-evident that Irish traditional music had finally migrated beyond its old communal settings and entered the realm of popular culture. At the same time, national education and media planners were taking a discerning interest in its future. Flagship programmes like RTE's '*Mo Cheol Thú*', 'Céilí House', 'Bring Down the Lamp', 'The Long Note' and 'The Pure Drop' presented traditional music in a manner which was both respectful to the tradition-bearer and astutely aware of his changing environment. Teachers too were making reels and jigs part of their school curriculum – for the first time since the foundation of the state. One of the first school teachers to break the 'high art' mould of music education in Ireland was Frank Custy who began teaching traditional music to his pupils in Toonagh National School in Co Clare in 1963. Frustrated by the failure of his curriculum to nurture the music of the indigenous hinterland, Custy learned traditional music from the celebrated Aughrim Slopes fiddler Jack Mulkere. Since 1963, he has taught thousands of adults as well as younger students, among them flute players Sean Conway and Garry Shannon, and fiddlers James Cullinan, Tola Custy and Bernie Whelan. His pupils went on to form groups like Stockton's Wing, The Mary Custy Band and Dísirt Tola which first brought accordion superstar Sharon Shannon to the attention of international audiences.

JOE COOLEY'S RETURN TO IRELAND

A few days before Christmas in 1973, the legendary accordionist Joe Cooley was laid to rest in his native Peterswell, Co Galway. Six months earlier, Cooley had come home from San Francisco, where Kevin Keegan, Joe Murtagh and himself had played Irish music through the golden age of the hippie revolution. Cooley returned to east Galway like a musical messiah returning to a long-lost congregation after twenty-seven years in the United States. Back home in Ireland, his music survived only in the memory of listeners who had heard him in the 1950s; and in the steps of dancers who had 'lifted' to the awesome swing of his 'Skylark'. In the summer and autumn of 1973, Cooley's music, accompanied by the banjo playing of Des Mulkere, filled the small pubs of Clare and Galway, while his fans relived again the *draíocht* of kitchen sets. Two years after his death, the first and only commercial recording of Joe Cooley's music reached the Irish consumer.

In some respects, Cooley's untimely passing marked the end of one era and the birth of another. With him, and others like him, went an age-old practice of storing 'great music' exclusively in the collective memory of local communities. Tape recorders now augmented the oral process, and mass commercial recordings of Irish traditional music became more commonplace. Throughout the 1970s and 1980s, the commercial life of traditional music became intense and competitive. As new concepts of cultural economics and heritage tourism began to emerge, traditional musicians, singers and dancers became marketing icons for the Irish tourist industry. Traditional music became the most popular form of entertainment sought out by foreign visitors to Ireland. Traditional music was also harnessed by other commercial forces. Beverage companies anxious to attract pint drinkers became acutely aware of the social magnetism of the pub session. Their lead was soon followed by other sponsors from industries which had little in common with traditional music. The commercial nexus reached its apogée when the transnational music industry expanded its portfolio of Irish traditional music ventures in the 1980s.

SUPER GROUPS AND CELEBRITIES

While many older musicians were disturbed by what they regarded as the 'melodic murder' of the set dance 'The King of the Fairies' by Celtic rock groups in the 1970s, there is little doubt that other ascendant stars of the music industry did much to focus popular attention on Irish traditional music. The past twenty-five years witnessed a succession of new musical liaisons, within which traditional music gelled with rock music, contemporary folk, as well as American and Eastern European folk musics. The sparking influence in this creative process was undoubtedly the group Planxty, which featured the uilleann piping of Liam Óg Ó Floinn merging with the Balkan rhythms of the bouzouki (first introduced to Irish music by Johnny Moynihan and Andy Irvine in the late 1960s) and singers Christy Moore, Donal Lunny and Andy Irvine. In 1973, the Galway group De Danann arrived on the scene. This time bouzouki combined with fiddle, played by Alec Finn and Frankie Gavin respectively. They were joined by accordionist and banjo player Charlie Piggott, *bodhrán* player Johnny 'Ringo' McDonagh and singer Dolores Keane. The next ten years saw De Danann undergo various line-up changes. Among the new arrivals were singers Maura O'Connell, Tim Lyons, Mary Black, Johnny Moynihan, Andy Irvine and Eleanor Shanley.

The arrival of The Bothy Band in 1975 was described by one critic as being 'instantly lethal'. Their exhilarating music was rhythmically powerful, melodically fast and dynamically blended. Their combination of talent included Paddy Keenan on pipes, singer Tríona Ní

Dhomhnaill on keyboard, Matt Molloy on flute, Mícheál Ó Domhnaill on guitar, Donal Lunny on bouzouki and Paddy Glackin on fiddle (later replaced by Tommy Peoples). While Planxty, De Danann and The Bothy Band made a dramatic impact on both Irish and international audiences in the 1970s, a plethora of other groups vied for popular attention during the following decade. These included Stockton's Wing, Any Old Time, Stocker's Lodge, Buttons and Bows, Patrick Street and Skylark. Other more eclectic configurations had also entered the marketplace, among them Clannad and Moving Hearts. Clannad evolved from an Irish-speaking family group in west Donegal, which included now-international superstar Enya. It combined Irish traditional music and songs with jazz and contemporary folk. Their ethereal magical sound went on to form the basis of 'New Age' Celtic music. Moving Hearts, which featured pipers Declan Masterson and Davy Spillane, had a very short life in the commercial circuit. The brainchild of Donal Lunny and Christy Moore, the ensemble attempted to fuse traditional music with contemporary electric rock. Unable to survive in the volatile world of 'rock economics', however, Moving Hearts left the scene in September 1984.

If the 1970s and 1980s were years of experimentation and coalescence, the 1990s have been marked to some degree by a return to the regional source of Irish traditional music. This is particularly evident in the melodic style and repertoire of the west Donegal group Altan. Combining authentic *sean nós* songs with highly polished instrumental performances, Altan has emerged as one of the most successful Irish super-groups performing on the international circuit today. A similar return to the regional wellspring of traditional music has been adopted by the Sligo-based group Dervish and the Galway-based Arcady.

Solo performers have also created dedicated

international audiences during the past twenty years. These include accordionists Joe Burke, Máirtín O'Connor, Jackie Daly, Sharon Shannon and Séamus Begley, concertina player Noel Hill, fiddlers Kevin Burke and James Kelly, and uilleann piper Ronan Browne. Among the most lauded is fiddler Martin Hayes whose music derives from a unique regional dialect of fiddling from the mountains of east Clare. After playing alongside his father PJ Hayes in the Tulla Céilí Band in the 1970s, Hayes moved to the United States in 1983. Since then, he has entertained audiences all over North America, Europe and Australia. Influenced by jazz musicians like the late Stéphane Grappelli, Hayes's music has created a forum for the ethereal listening rhythms of east Clare and east Galway, which were often marginalised in the fast-paced music of the marketplace. Keenly aware of his traditional background, Hayes confides that 'many of the old musicians had this special *draíocht*. Some of them weren't technical virtuosos, but through the honesty of their expression, they could touch your heart. It is this quality that has driven and inspired me all of my musical life.'

While Irish traditional music was being entwined with rock and contemporary folk music in the 1980s, other innovative alliances were being forged with classical composers who were venturing beyond the 'high-art' sanctuary of their predecessors. In the resulting interchange, a number of orchestral works emerged which incorporated traditional performers. The piping of Liam Óg Ó Floinn and the music of composer Shaun Davey came together in *The Brendan Voyage*, *The Pilgrim, Granuaile*, and *The Relief of the Siege of Derry*. Mícheál Ó Súilleabháin's three-movement suite *Oileán/Island* brought traditional flute player Matt Molloy together with the Irish Chamber Orchestra. In 1991, fiddler Charlie Lennon, who grew up within a vibrant community of traditional musicians in Co Leitrim, released his *Island Wedding*, a work in sixteen movements for traditional instruments and orchestra. The 1990s saw further works from Charlie Lennon and from the young Clare composer Patrick Cassidy.

Folk theatre too created international audiences for Irish traditional music during the 1980s. Spurred by the take-off of cultural tourism, especially in the West of Ireland, theatrical ensembles like Siamsa Tíre in Tralee, Co Kerry, and later on Brú Boru in Cashel, Co Tipperary, developed stage performances based on traditional rural themes re-enacted through mime, music, song and dance. The 1993 'Midnight Court' production, adapted by singer Seán Tyrrell from Brian Merriman's epic poem, was a more avant garde exercise in folk theatre.

IRISH TRADITIONAL MUSIC IN EUROPE

Despite the romantic assumptions of New Age Celts and the ulterior motives of recording companies, there is no historical overlap between Irish traditional music and the music of Brittany. Irish audiences became aware of Breton music in the 1970s mainly through the recordings of harper Alan Stivell. Since then, a steady stream of exchanges has taken place between musicians from both traditions. Breton festivals like those held in Lorient, Douarnenez and Paimpol frequently invite Irish musicians to perform. Similarly, festival gatherings in Ireland attracted musicians from Brittany. In the 1980s, these cross-cultural exchanges created a forum for groups like Kornog from Brittany, and in more recent times, The House Band, whose *biniou* and *bombarde* player John Skelton has a deep understanding of both Irish and Breton traditions.

Ireland's entry into the EEC helped to open new tourist channels with the European mainland. During the following decade, Ireland became inundated by music lovers from Europe heading west towards music sessions and *fleadhanna*. This traffic also created a market for Irish music in Germany, Belgium, Italy, the Netherlands and Scandinavia. Heading the resulting export of Irish talent were groups like Clannad and The Chieftains. Celebrated solo performers like Micko Russell were also patronised by European audiences.

Apart from hosting touring musicians from Ireland, some European cities developed their own Irish music communities. Paris was by far the most impressive of these enclaves. For the past twenty years an Irish music and dance scene has been growing in the French capital. Throughout the 1980s, L'Association Irlandaise held regular music and set dancing classes at La Mission Bretonne in Montparnasse. Similarly, the Parisian branch of Na Píobairí Uilleann did much to promote uilleann piping all over France. Unlike many musicians who come to traditional music from outside its indigenous habitat, French performers have made an insightful effort to understand the dialectic source of Irish traditional music. Fiddlers like Vincent Blin, Patrick Ourceau and Michel Ferry, as well as flute player Hervé Cantal and piper Denis Kersual have a sensitive knowledge of the regional styles of Clare and east Galway. During the 1980s, they made several trips to Ireland to learn directly from older masters like Paddy Murphy, Bobby Casey, Paddy Canny and Junior Crehan.

DOOLIN: A MUSICAL MECCA

As the floodgates of tourism opened in the 1970s, the fishing village of Doolin, on the edge of the Burren in north Clare, became a musical mecca for multitudes of rucksacked travellers from Europe and North America. Escaping the chaos of urban life, many arrived in Ireland with little more than a hitchhiker's placard showing 'Doolin' penned in black ink. Since then, Doolin has hosted an unbroken session of music, begun by a few locals, who have long since ceded their place to visiting players from all over the world. Consisting of three pubs, a few hostels, an eclectic choice of restaurants, and a *bureau de change*, Doolin now has an 'alternative' multinational community which has integrated with an older indigenous population. Attracted by the relaxed rural lifestyle, many of the newcomers earn a modest living, as buskers or session musicians. Over sixty years ago, Jamesie Woods, a local Doolin character, was heard to proclaim, '*Ná bí a' caint,* we had a great night for a week'. He was describing a visit made to Doolin by the artist Augustus John and his bohemian friends Oliver St John Gogarty and Dylan Thomas. It seems that little has changed in the interim.

Long before Doolin became a traditional music mecca, it housed a rich store of folklore and music. In the 1930s when Doolin was an Irish-speaking district, Séamus Ó Duilearga collected a unique corpus of folklore from Doolin storyteller Stiofán Ó hEalaoire. During the same period, American anthropologists Conrad Arensberg and Solon Kimball conducted fieldwork in Doolin for their seminal study *Family and Community in Ireland.* In the 1940s, its musicians, such as Peadaí Pheaitín Ó Flannagáin, John and Paddy Killourhy, Willie Shannon and the Russell brothers, contributed a remarkable collection of dance tunes, songs and anecdotes to Séamus Ennis for the archives of the Folklore Commission. In more recent times, the Russell brothers were regarded as the musical high-priests of Doolin. Pakie, a stonemason and folk philosopher, was a concertina player with an exceptional knowledge of cross-key fingering and an uncommon repertoire of tunes and settings. His brother Micko, who played flute and whistle, was one of the last *sean nós* singers in Clare. A third brother Gussie still plays nightly in O'Connor's pub surrounded by scores of listeners. While the world came to Doolin to meet Pakie, his brother Micko took his music to the world. Starting with a few trips to Germany in the 1970s, Micko became a seasoned world traveller before his death in 1994. His deceptively simple music was laced with unpredictable melodic variations and an extensive store of archaic Clare settings. Undisturbed by huge audiences or language barriers, Micko was as comfortable performing in the National Concert Hall as he was playing for a half set on his own flagstone floor in Donagore.

THE WILLIE CLANCY SUMMER SCHOOL

Clare piper Willie Clancy was born on Christmas Eve 1918. He grew up in an environment that was rich in music, song and dance. As a child, his imagination was fired by stories told by the *seanchaí* and tunes played by his neighbours during their night-time *cuaird*. Both his parents played; his mother Ellen, the concertina, and his father Gilbert, the flute and concertina. Gilbert had inherited a wealth of music from the blind piper Garrett Barry, a native of Inagh, nine miles to the east of Miltown Malbay. Garrett was like an absent guest in Clancy's house, even though he had died penniless in the local workhouse nineteen years before Willie was born.

As a young man, Willie played the flute. His preference changed quickly, however, when he heard the uilleann pipes played for the first time by the travelling piper Johnny Doran. By 1938 he had acquired a bag and chanter from Johnny Doran's brother Felix. In 1947 he won first prize at the Oireachtas piping competition in Dublin. Willie's trade, like that of his father, was carpentry. After serving his time as an apprentice, he took to the road in the 1940s, first to Dublin and eventually to London. When his father died in 1957, he returned home to Miltown Malbay. That same year, he made his seminal 78rpm recordings for Gael Linn. His 'Old Bucks' and 'The Ravelled Hank of Yarn', played on a Maloney chanter made in Knockerra in 1860, are classics of Irish piping. For the next eighteen years Willie held court in Miltown Malbay, playing mainly in the kitchen of Friel's pub where he hosted pipers and singers, storytellers and raconteurs from all walks of life who came to enjoy his wit and company.

Shortly after Willie died on 24 January 1973, his friends Martin Talty, Junior Crehan, Seán Reid, Muiris Ó Rocháin, JC Talty and Harry Hughes decided to create a living monument to him in Miltown Malbay, rather than venerate his achievements with a cut-stone plaque. Consequently, the Willie Clancy Summer School was set up in July 1973. It started modestly, with eighty students and a small faculty. Twenty-five years later, it has become an international master's forum for Irish traditional music. Assembling one thousand students from over thirty different countries, and teachers from universities and performance stages all over the world, it caters for instrumental music, traditional singing and set dancing.

The director of the school since its inception in 1973 is Muiris Ó Rocháin, a native of Dingle, Co Kerry. Influenced by similar schools of traditional culture in Denmark, Ó Rocháin's driving philosophy was threefold – educational, cultural and social. He was acutely aware of the rich storehouse of indigenous culture that would be accessible to students coming to west Clare. The school is a primary meeting place for Na Píobairí Uilleann, the Irish pipers' association which Willie helped form in 1968. From the outset, this organisation has advocated the importance of learning traditional music for the sake of appreciating it, rather than treating it as a prelude to winning competitions. Throughout the week, its members – who travel from various Irish branches, as well as a network of international branches from Paris to Seattle – provide reedmaking sessions, piping workshops and classes. While hosting musicians from across the globe, the Willie Clancy Summer School also provides a forum for local masters like Michael Falsey, Bríd Donoghue, Mick Flynn, Gerdie Commane, Junior Crehan, Ollie Conway and Marty

O'Keefe. Similarly, its example has inspired other schools all over the West of Ireland.

SEAN NÓS SINGING: RECENT HISTORY

Sean nós singing has sustained a vibrant audience since the 1960s, especially within Gaeltacht communities where it can be appreciated by listeners familiar with its subtleties and regional variations. The dialects of *sean nós* identified by Seán Ó Riada in 1962 in his Radio Éireann series 'Our Musical Heritage' still prevail today, although not without some changes to repertoires and quality of songs. The Munster tradition in west Cork has experienced its own renaissance in recent decades, not least as a result of Ó Riada's influence in the Cúil Aodha Gaeltacht. Singers like Iarla Ó Lionáird and the late Diarmuid Ó Súilleabháin have helped to sustain songs like *'Cath Chéim an Fhia'* and *'A Mháire Ní Laoire'* which were sung by *sean nós* masters like Pádraig Ó Tuama and Máire Ní Cheocháin. In the Déise Gaeltacht of Co Waterford, *sean nós* singer Áine Uí Cheallaigh carries on an indigenous dialect which was exemplified by Nioclás Tóibín, whose renditions of *'Na Connerys'* and *'An Buachaillín Bán'* have become *sean nós* classics. In west Munster, the Corca Dhuibhne songs of Seán de hÓra, and those of the Blasket Island singers, have passed on to another generation of local singers, among them the Begleys from Baile na bPoc.

The Gaeltacht community of Ráth Cairn, Co Meath, has also had its *sean nós* master. Darach Ó Catháin, whose people came to Ráth Cairn from Connemara, left a rich legacy of *sean nós* material, not least *'An Sceilpín Draighneach'* and *'Donncha Bán'*. The Donegal dialect has also come to prominence, especially in the singing of Mairéad Ní Dhomhnaill, Lillis Ó Laoire and Mairéad Ní Mhaonaigh who have helped focus attention on the songs of Róise Rua Nic Gríanna from Arranmore, as well as the songs of Neilí Ní Dhónaill.

The Connemara Gaeltacht has proven to be the most enduring heartland of the *sean nós* tradition. Celebrated masters like Colm Ó Caoidheáin, Seosamh Ó hÉanaí, Seán 'ac Dhonncha, Máire Áine Nic Dhonnchadha, Sorcha Ní Ghuairim, Josie Sheáin Jack Mac Donncha, Seán Ó Conaire and Johnny Mháirtín Learaí Mac Donncha have left an astonishing legacy of *sean nós* materials on disc and in various archive collections in Ireland and in the United States. Ó hÉanaí, who spent over twenty years working in Brooklyn, was an artist-in-residence at the University of Washington in Seattle before his death in 1984. The university archive contains a considerable collection of 'Éinniú's' songs and folklore. Dara Bán Mac Donnchadha from Aird Thoir, Carna, is considered by many to be the finest living *sean nós* singer in Ireland today. His neighbour and friend Seosamh Ó hÉanaí was known to have remarked that 'this man is better than myself'. Other *sean nós* singers from Connemara have followed Ó hÉanaí's path into exile in cosmopolitan America, among them Áine Meenaghan in Chicago, and Bridget Fitzgerald and Máirín Uí Chéide in Boston, all continue to promote his songs.

A number of factors have combined to sustain the popularity of *sean nós*, particularly within Gaeltacht communities. It is featured almost on a daily basis by Raidió na Gaeltachta, the Gaeltacht areas radio service, which has created a vibrant system of communication between the various Irish language dialects. It has also found its way onto an extensive series of commercial recordings in recent years. The Connemara-based company Cló-Iar Chonnachta is the most active promoter of *sean nós* songs and singers throughout the West of Ireland. *Sean nós* is also promoted by various singers' clubs and cultural organisations, especially the Góilín traditional singers' club in Dublin, as well as Sean Nós Cois Life (*'Sean Nós* by the Liffey'). The Willie Clancy

Summer School and Scoil Éigse (organised by Comhaltas in conjunction with the All Ireland *Fleadh*) also devote considerable attention to *sean nós* workshops and performances. Similarly, the research work of Ríonach Uí Ógáin, Séamus Mac Mathúna and Bairbre Ní Fhloinn in recent years has raised the level of public (and academic) appreciation of *sean nós*. Perhaps the most significant catalyst in the revival of *sean nós* has been the coveted *Corn Uí Riada* prize which singers compete for at the annual Oireachtas na Gaeilge arts festival. This prestigious competition has been dominated by Connemara singers in recent decades, among them Tomás Mac Eoin, Treasa Ní Mhiolláin, John Sheáin Dharach Seoighe as well as Nóra, Sarah and Nan Ghriallais, three of eleven sisters from Muiceanach-Idir-Dhá-Sháile. In November 1995 a remarkable exception occurred in this Gaeltacht-dominated contest; Dublin singer Mairéad Ní Oistín won the ultimate Oireachtas prize for her renditions of '*Donncha Bán*' and '*Barr an tSléibhe*'. This was the first time a native Dubliner won *Corn Uí Riada* – a fact which bodes well for the future of Ireland's most delicate and archaic song tradition.

SET DANCING SINCE 1970

Despite a history of indifference from the official guardians of Irish dance, set dancing has undergone an astounding revival in recent decades. In 1971, the GAA incorporated set dancing into its *Scór* competitions, a stage talent series involving hurling and football clubs from all over Ireland. This was the first serious attempt to create any kind of national forum for set dancers. Its impact was felt immediately in rural communities as troupes of set dancers, complete with uniforms, competed against rival sets in local pub contests and parish festivals. The Mullagh and Quilty sets from Clare were to the fore in this early revival. Sets from other traditional bastions like Sliabh Luachra, Ballycommon and Cashel were also active. Set dancers were included as part of the Irish music delegation which travelled to the Smithsonian Institute in Washington in 1976 to commemorate the American War of Independence. Master set dancers Willie Keane and Ollie Conway treated American audiences to steps they were taught by Pat Barron, the last of the travelling dancing masters to teach in west Clare in the 1940s. In 1978, Comhaltas Ceoltóirí Éireann began to organise set competitions, initially as part of their *Fleadh Nua* schedule and later on, as part of their main *Fleadh* programme. Drawing on master set dancers like Martin and Bridie Burns, and Paddy Queally, the Willie Clancy Summer School began to teach set dancing in 1982. Slógadh, a national arts competition for young people, also incorporated sets.

Another revival occurred in the 1980s, this time in urban Ireland. As quiet sessions in inner-city pubs gave way to set dancers, gym kits and fast music, set dance classes and clubs developed among a whole new generation of urban, middle class enthusiasts. While styles and debates varied between more traditional forms of the 'slide in' and newer form of the 'batter', several older sets like 'The Paris Set' and 'The Clare Lancers' were revived from the oral recollections of master set dancers like Dan Furey, and Joe and Biddy MacNamara. During the past twenty years, set dancing historians Terry Moylan in Dublin and Larry Lynch in San Francisco have produced seminal studies on traditional set dancing styles. Similarly, dancing masters Joe and Siobhán O'Donovan from Cork, Pádraig O'Dea from Clare, Mick Mulkearns from Galway, and the late Connie Ryan from Tipperary have travelled all over North America teaching set dancing. The revival of sets has been paralleled by a rejuvenation of céilí band music. Among the céilí bands who play regularly for sets are: The Tulla, The Kilfenora, The Shaskeen, The Bridge, The Moving Cloud, and The Temple House, as well as The Matt Cunningham and Seán Norman Céilí Bands.

THE RIVERDANCE PHENOMENON

Since the founding of the North American Feis Commission in 1968, the United States and Canada have turned out thousands of young Irish step dancers who compete in a myriad of *feiseanna* from New York to San Francisco, Dallas to Toronto, every year. The most talented travel to Ireland to compete at the World Championship dancing competitions. Among the luminaries to pass through this system during the past twenty years were Donny Golden, Jean Butler and Liam Harney. The undisputed genius of this pantheon, however, was Michael Flatley, the first American-born dancer to win an All-World Championship.

Born in Chicago of Irish parents, Flatley grew up in a city that was well-endowed with Irish traditional music. In addition to a career in dance, he also became an accomplished flute player in an ambience where he had access to traditional masters like Eleanor Neary, 'Cuz' Teehan, Liz Carroll and Johnny McGreevy. Flatley's talents were showcased by the Chieftains on numerous international tours. The youngest-ever recipient of a National Heritage Fellowship, he was recognised by the National Endowment for the Arts as one of America's most eminent performers, and, in 1991, the National Geographic Society declared him 'a living treasure'. Flatley danced his way into the *Guinness Book of World Records* for his tapping speed. All of this irrepressible talent, tradition and energy ultimately exploded onto the world stage as *Riverdance*.

Produced and choreographed as an interlude performance during the 1994 Eurovision Song Contest, *Riverdance* featured the music of Bill Whelan and the step dancing of Michael Flatley and Jean Butler. This interlude act became such a phenomenal success that it was expanded into a full-length theatrical production, combining modern compositions and choral work, with dance forms from Ireland, Spain, Russia and the United States. It subsequently performed to packed houses in North America, Europe and Australia. Its runaway success has led to the creation of multiple casts which employ scores of Irish dancers, singers and musicians.

While *Riverdance* put Irish step dancing onto the map of popular culture, Michael Flatley's breakaway production *Lord of the Dance* took Irish music and dance to unprecedented theatrical heights in 1996. Using a dazzling display of cinematographic effects and a precarious composite of mythological motifs, *Lord of the Dance* featured a battalion of step dancers, with Flatley dancing as well as playing concert flute. Unlike its precursor, this production incorporated genuine dance music and figure dances from the living tradition.

Riverdance and *Lord of the Dance* have both generated a paradigm shift in Irish step dancing. Since 1994, this formulaic bastion of national dance has changed from an old competitive world of medals and *feiseanna*, to a new commercial milieu of theatrical extravaganza. In the resulting cocktail of Celtic twilight and Broadway panache, Tin Pan Alley and Hollywood, Irish musicians and dancers, like their vaudevillian predecessors, are retailoring their art for a radically new and intensely competitive international stage.

CONTINUITY AND CHANGE IN THE 1990S

Although there has been a dramatic renaissance in Irish traditional music in recent decades, it has not taken place without reflection and controversy. Throughout the 1990s, there has been much debate about continuity and change, purism and innovation in Irish traditional music. The subject of conferences and various media exchanges, this debate has been fuelled mainly by the growing commercialisation of Irish traditional music, which has marginalised local as well as older performers and styles in Ireland and North America.

For older players, the renaissance of recent decades has seen the traditional emphasis on old-style melodic performance undermined by excessive harmonic and percussive accompaniment. Although there were earlier precedents, many traced this transition to the emergence of super groups in the 1970s who introduced guitars, bouzoukis, double-basses, bongos and electronic synthesisers into an older acoustic world of fiddles, flutes and uilleann pipes. While these new arrivals did much to initiate change and innovation, many of the subtleties implicit in older styles of melodic performance were lost beneath a tide of fast and insensitive accompaniment. The renaissance has also witnessed an increased separation between 'performance' music and 'dance' music. Older players, whose sense of rhythm was implicitly linked to set dancing, often felt isolated by younger players who abandoned the traditional dance milieu for the concert stage and television studio. Linked implicitly to this was a lack of familiarity between modern step dancers and musicians. Trained almost exclusively for competitions, step dancers had minimal contact with live music. When this occurred at *feiseanna*, musicians were required to play dance tunes in rigid time signatures set by *feis* authorities – a practice which had no precedent in traditional dancing. The dislocation of *sean nós* melodies from their Irish language lyrics also became a contentious issue. New Age Celtic artists in the 1990s focused renewed attention on Irish language songs. However, their orchestrated and ethereal treatment of *sean nós* melodies had little in common with the version sung in Gaeltacht communities. This transition resulted in a shift away from indigenous *sean nós* sources, especially by younger players who preferred to improvise liberally with these revered melodies, rather than conform to their authentic Gaeltacht settings.

Since the 1980s, most traditional musicians in Ireland

have been affected by the dramatic commercialisation of their music by corporate sponsors as well as media and recording companies. While some embraced this change, others chose to remain circumspect. In the transition from the traditional to the professional domain, younger players were quick to endorse the festival circuit and the career of the celebrity, while many older players were deeply disturbed by the fact that multimedia entrepreneurs were packaging Irish traditional music for mammoth television audiences – with little regard for the legitimate integrity of the tradition. Many traditional singers resented the fact that popular music celebrities, with no competency in the Irish language, could record hit songs in Irish, which they learnt phonetically. Others were concerned that performers and companies with no previous connections to Irish music were rapidly producing 'Celtic' albums and videos to capitalise on the global market created by *Riverdance*, and forging commericial links with African, Cajun and other World Music genres with no basis in Irish music history. To further compound matters, a new coterie of journalists began to critique Irish traditional music in the 1990s, some of whom were acquainted with the living tradition, while others had no performance knowledge of the music, and knew little about its tradition-bearers or their lifestyles.

The debate about purism and innovation in Irish traditional music was also fuelled by a series of controversial media productions in the 1990s. Each had its own philosophical impact on avid consumer audiences in Ireland and North America. In 1991 the lavish multimedia package 'Bringing It All Back Home' explored Irish music in America. While focusing primarily on the professional marketplace, the series attempted to forge a series of musical connections between Irish traditional music and several genres of music in contemporary America. In 1993 'From Shore to Shore', a documentary produced by

Patrick Mullins, explored the history of Irish traditional music in New York City. A well-researched and sensitive production, it featured the music of Paddy Reynolds, Andy McGann, Martin Wynne, Tom Doherty, Maureen Connolly, and other New York musicians. In 1994 Tony MacMahon's 'Come West Along the Road' revisited many of the RTE programmes made since the 1960s. Devoid of the glitter of the commercial stage, this production was a rare paragon of authenticity. It contained some unique footage from the early *fleadhanna* featuring notable figures like Willie Clancy and Joe Leary, the Tulla Céilí Band and the renowned dancing master Paddy Bán Ó Broin. In 1995 'A River of Sound' explored the relationship between Irish traditional music and other World Music genres. This 'modernist' series proved to be extremely controversial and provoked much polarised debate among Irish traditional musicians. While making the general public aware of the evolutionary process within Irish traditional music, it left many older musicians feeling sceptical and apprehensive about the future of their own music-making.

As the commercialisation of Irish traditional music gathered pace throughout the 1990s, the vexed issues of copyright and ownership have become increasingly important. What had once been a communal folk art was quickly becoming a privatised market commodity, controlled by recording companies, media moguls and a bevy of agents, promoters and marketing gurus. As folk art is still awaiting copyright legislation, Irish traditional music has been considered (for the most part) to be within the domain of common property. Although some traditional players were folk composers in their own right, few chose to copyright their compositions formally. On the other hand, intellectual property lawyers rallied to protect the recordings of professional artists, who made minor alterations to traditional songs and tunes before committing them to tape. While these alterations may have qualified as private property, the practice undermined the integrity of the traditional storehouse. In 1990, ethnomusicologist Hugh Shields likened this practice to the 'private enclosure of common land'. Eight years afterwards, the legal status of the traditional performer still remains precarious, not least because his music predates the profit dynamics of the music industry, and continues to be defined within a collective oral environment.

The relationship between traditional music and its corporate sponsors also added to the perplexities of continuity and change in the 1990s. While most sporting and cultural events in Ireland depended on corporate philanthropy, many traditional musicians were disturbed by the marketing ethics of drinks companies and car manufacturers who sponsored traditional music events. Throughout the 1990s, purists questioned the motives of drinks companies which issued lists of 'official pub sessions' to tourists arriving in Ireland. Their peers in the United States disputed the fact that the term *'fleadh'* (which had been associated with communal festivals since the 1950s) was now being used as a marketing vehicle encompassing all types of professional entertainment. Conversely, innovators and administrators within the traditional domain regarded corporate sponsorship as a necessary prerequisite to stage national festivals which helped safeguard the future of the living tradition.

QUO VADIS? THE FUTURE OF THE TRADITION

The popularity of Irish traditional music at the present time is certainly without precedent. As a performance art, it has become accessible to television and concert audiences all over the world. In Ireland and North America, the vision of Comhaltas Ceoltóirí Éireann has continued to flourish in its *fleadhanna*, classes and concert tours. Similarly, its Irish Folk Orchestra, which includes young performers from Ireland and Britain, has come to fruition under the direction of flutist Mícheál Ó hAlmhain. Visitors to Ireland now come equipped with directories of music sessions and road maps to summer schools like the Cairdeas na bhFidléirí in Glencolmcille, Co Donegal, and the Willie Clancy Summer School in Miltown Malbay, Co Clare. Americans who fail to reach these events can learn from many of the same teachers at the Catskills Irish Arts Week in upstate New York and the Swannanoa Gathering in North Carolina.

The increased participation of young people in Irish traditional music bodes very well for its future. Young musicians, singers and dancers growing up in Ireland have access to hundreds of master performers, as well as opportunities to study traditional music in second and third level institutions. Their peers in Boston, New York and St Louis also enjoy access to master performers and educational opportunities. Of equal importance is the growth of research resources that attract students to Irish traditional music. In Ireland the archive work of Nicholas Carolan and Séamus Mac Mathúna as well as the field recordings of Peter Browne, Harry Bradshaw and Caoimhín Mac Aoidh have added significantly to the store of research materials available to students of the music. Similar work by Séamus Connolly, Philippe Varlet, Bill Ochs and Mick Maloney has added considerably to Irish music resources in North America.

Goodwill towards the music continues to abound, even in the most unlikely circles. The internet, for example, has now become a forum for Irish traditional music news groups – despite a welter of uninformed dialogue at times. The extended Irish community in North America has also become acutely aware of its US-based traditional performers, among them, fiddlers James Kelly and Martin Hayes, accordionists Paddy O'Brien, James Keane and

Patricia Kenneally, pipers Jerry O'Sullivan and Willie Kelly as well as singers Áine Meenaghan and Robbie O'Connell. One of the significant outcomes of the present upsurge in Irish traditional music has been a renewed liaison with the traditional music of Scotland and Cape Breton Island. Irish fiddlers Antóin Mac Gabhann and Máire O'Keefe have both recorded with Cape Breton musicians, while fiddlers Tommy Peoples and Alasdair Fraser continue to explore the archaic Gaelic roots that Irish and Scottish music-makers shared over two centuries ago.

As its rich and diverse history has shown, Irish traditional music has always experienced change and has been enriched by centuries of innovation. As it evolves into another new century, it will continue to converge with other musical genres, interface with modern technologies, and reach out to unfamiliar audiences. What remains uncertain is how these oncoming forces will affect the music makers themselves. The present purism of some traditional players reflects the strained interface between popular culture, which is absorbing their music, and traditional culture, whence it came. Above all, their purism has grown out of a sincere concern for the regional and traditional aspects of Irish culture. As long as these guardians of Irish traditional music are duly revered by their heirs, and the integrity of their oral tradition respected by all of its recipients, there is no reason why circumspect purism and perceptive innovation cannot co-exist in the new millennium.

GLOSSARY OF TRADITIONAL MUSIC TERMS

aisling: Irish for 'vision' or 'dream'; eighteenth-century visionary poem.

amhrán: Irish for 'song'; songs in accented metres common after the decline of bardic schools.

bean a'tí: literally 'woman of the house', hostess of a house session or dance.

broadside: sheet printed on one side; popular ballads were usually distributed on broadsides.

caoineadh: Irish for 'lament', of which there are several different types in the Irish song tradition.

carol: mediaeval lyric song and dance, brought to Ireland by the Normans.

céilí: a 'traditional dance', hence *céilí* band, also referred to as rambling or *scoraíocht*.

craic: 'fun' or 'entertainment'. The term is of dubious origin.

cuaird: a social visit to a neighbour's house, often involving storytelling and music.

dán: poem.

dinnsheanchas: traditional placename lore, often carried in the names of tunes or songs.

duanaire: book of poems or songs, generally dedicated to a Gaelic overlord or family.

fear a'tí: literally 'man of the house'; host or master of ceremonies at a house session or dance.

feis/feiseanna: primarily a step dance festival.

fleadh cheoil/fleadhanna: festival of music, organised by Comhaltas Ceoltóirí Eireann.

gaeltacht: an Irish-speaking district or community, mostly on the Atlantic seaboard.

jig: traditional dance tune in 6/8 or 9/8 time; also a step dance.

lilting: singing dance music to vocables; also referred to as 'mouth music' or *portaireacht*.

meitheal: a group of cooperative farm workers. Their work usually ended with a dance.

oíche cheoil: a night of music, song and dance, held in halls or kitchens.

polka: traditional dance tune in 2/4 time; also a common set dance type in Cork and Kerry.

reacaire: reciter or singer at the court of a Gaelic lord; associated with the poet and harper.

reel: traditional dance tune in 4/4 time, used commonly for sets and step dancing.

draíocht: Irish for 'magic'; commonly used to describe an ethereal quality in traditional music.

sean nós: 'old style'; unaccompanied singing in Irish, the apex of the living tradition.

sean nós **dancing**: old style traditional dancing, with a loose upper body and intricate 'low to the floor' steps.

scoraíocht: an 'evening visit' to a neighbour's house for music and song; see also *cuaird*.

seanchas: 'traditional lore'; involves folk tales, legends, folk wisdom, songs, etc.

set dancing: traditional group dancing based on quadrille figures, common since early 1800s.

swaree: from the French *soirée* (evening festivities); used in Clare to refer to house dancing.

MUSIC, SONG AND DANCE COLLECTIONS

Breandán Breathnach *Ceol Rince na hEireann,* (Vols. 1, 2, 3 and 4), (Dublin, 1963-96)

Francis O'Neill *The Dance Music of Ireland: 1001 Gems,* (Dublin, 1907)

Hugh Shields Shamrock, *Rose & Thistle: Folk Singing in North Derry,* (Belfast, 1981)

John P Cullinane *Aspects of the History of Irish Dancing,* (Cork, 1987)

TRADITIONAL MUSIC ORGANISATIONS

Comhaltas Ceoltóirí Eireann
    32 Belgrave Square
    Monkstown, Co Dublin
    Tel: (353 – 1) 661 1840

Conradh na Gaeilge (Gaelic League)
    6 Harcourt Street
    Dublin 2
    Tel: (353 – 1) 875 7401

Irish Traditional Music Archive
    63 Merrion Square
    Dublin 2
    Tel: (353 – 1) 661 9696

Na Píobairí Uilleann
    15 Henrietta Street
    Dublin 1
    Tel: (353 – 1) 873 0093

Ceolas: Celtic Music Internet
Source
Stanford University,
California
http://celtic.stanford.edu/
ceolas.html

SELECT DISCOGRAPHY

Darach Ó Catháin *Traditional Irish Unaccompanied Singing*, Shanachie 34005

Joe Heaney (Seosamh Ó hEanaí) *Irish Traditional Songs in Gaelic & English*, Ossian OSS22

Máire Áine Ní Dhonnchadha *Deora Aille*, Claddagh CC6 – 1970

Various Singers *More Grand Airs from Connemara*, Ossian OSS43 – 1991

Mary Ann Carolan *Songs in the Irish Tradition*, Topic 12TS362

Willie Clancy *The Minstrel from Clare*, Topic 12T175

Joe Cooley *Cooley*, Gael Linn CEF044 – 1975

Séamus Ennis *The Best of Irish Piping*, TARACD 1002/9

Paddy Canny *Traditional Music from the Legendary East Clare Fiddler*, CICD 129

Joe Ryan *An Buachaill Dreoite*, Cló Iar-Chonnachta CICD 113

John Doherty *Bundle and Go* Green Linnet GLCD 3077

Tommy Potts *The Liffey Banks*, Claddagh CC13

Pádraig O'Keefe *Sliabh Luachra Fiddle Master*, RTE CD174

Robbie Hannon *Traditional Irish Music played on the Uilleann Pipes*, Claddagh 4CC53

Boston College *Irish Fiddle Festival My Love is in America*, Green Linnet GLCD 1110

Irish Fiddle Masters from the 78RPM Era *Milestone at the Garden*, Rounder CD 1123

Various Ensembles & Solo Artists *Irish Dance Music*, Topic TSCD602

Mairéad Ní Mhaonaigh & Frankie Kennedy *Ceol Aduaidh*, Gael Linn CEFCD102

Mick O'Brien *May Morning Dew*, ACM CD101

Mary Bergin *Feadóga Stáin*, (Vols. 1&2) Gael Linn CEF071 & Gael Linn CEF 149

Martin Hayes *Martin Hayes*, Green Linnet GLCD 1127

Ronan Browne and Peter O'Loughlin *The South West Wind*, Claddagh 4CC47

Gearóid Ó hAllmhuráin *Traditional Music from Clare & Beyond*, Celtic Crossings OWR0046

The Kilfenora Céilí Band *Set on Stone: Traditional Dance Music from Ireland*, TOLCD1

The Bothy Band *1975*, Mulligan LUN 002

A NOTE ON SESSION ETIQUETTE

Every year, thousands of people attend traditional music sessions all over Ireland. These sessions take place in city bars, on street corners during *fleadhanna*, and in small rural pubs. To the stranger or visiting musician, the session may seem like a haphazard affair which stops and starts without any apparent logic. However, each session has its own internal logic, social code and sense of time, all of which vary from one setting to the next. The following set of pointers should help the visiting musician, as well as the listener, to enjoy the session and, hopefully, to come to terms with some of the unspoken subtleties of Irish social life.

Most pubs reserve special seating areas for musicians. These will usually be self-evident on arrival and should not be occupied by the visitors, unless they are invited specifically by the most senior musicians. *Bodhrán* players should use discretion when 'sitting in' to sessions. A 'quiet' peripheral role is always appreciated by experienced musicians. If a second *bodhrán* player is present, it is usually a good idea for one player to take a break, rather than have both *bodhráns* play together. A similar practice holds for guitars and other harmony instruments.

Every session has a key or a number of key players. The standard practice in the West of Ireland is to defer to the oldest player in the session. He or she usually starts each set of tunes, sets the rhythm and pace of the music (which should be respected scrupulously) and decides on the combination of tunes to be played during any one set.

Sessions generally consist of dance music, but may also involve an occasional solo song, or dance. It is usually considered polite to wait until one is invited before giving a solo performance. The interlude between tunes is an important opportunity for conversation, and for learning names of tunes and sources. It is impolite for the unacquainted stranger to interrupt this ritual to give a solo performance. However, when solo performances – especially songs – are taking place, an attentive silence is always appreciated.

Although sessions are usually held in a public place, most musicians are uncomfortable when members of the audience record their music on video tape or audio recorders. Many musicians feel that this intrudes on the intimacy of the gathering and steals the *draíocht* of the music. It is most impolite to record without the explicit permission of the musicians, most of whom will give it in any case. It is extremely impolite to record a session with a concealed tape recorder. This constitutes an act of musical piracy.

Finally, Ciarán Carson, in his wisdom, has suggested that the best form of appreciation for the music is to buy a 'discreet drink' for the musicians. He is absolutely right! Enjoy the music!